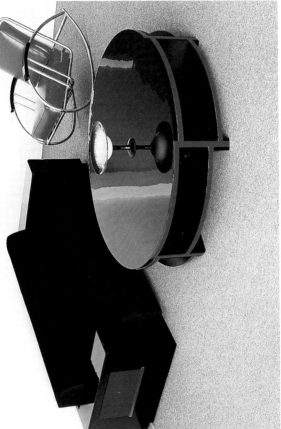

Bob & Stephanie
A guide to help you
fill your new home 29th Annual Edition
with old treasures • Published every April
Enjoy ☺ *Kathleen & Frank*
Lopez

Taylor's Guide to

ANTIQUE SHOPS

In Illinois
& Southern Wisconsin

1997

The Guide to
• Suburban, City & Country Shops
• "Hard-to-Find" Repair People, Services
and Replacement Parts
• Antique Shows

Irene Taylor, publisher
•

MOONLIGHT PRESS
202 N. Brighton Pl., Arlington Heights, IL 60004

Phone: 847 / 392-8438 • Fax: 847 / 392-8312

FIRST MESA

AMERICAN INDIAN ART
PREHISTORIC ARTIFACTS
BOOKS

Specializing in:

Pottery · Basketry · Weavings · Flint · Stone Tools
Ceremonials · Pipes · Beadwork · Fetishes
Ornamentals · Masks · Weaponry · Primitives
Geological Specimens · Fossils · Horns · Skulls
Bones · Mounts · Antiquities · Tribal Art · Folk Art
Kachinas · Sculptures · Jewelry · Paintings
Americana · Pre-Columbian Art

Please see opposite page for information on our Artifact Catalog

April, 1997

Gentle Antiquer,

Taylor's Guide exists for one reason—to launch you into the right direction, even into another dimension. So grab your guide and step into the past. It takes you back to a simpler time. Memories can be refreshed - one of the reasons you love antiques.

Research is part of the interest. Now the Wisconsin Antique Dealers Association (WADA) is offering 21 videos about antiques. Check their ad on page 72.

We have indexed those offering repairs and services in the "Hard-to-Find" Index starting on page 19. And on page 257 is the start of the list of antiques found in the shops of the advertisers. Of course, we couldn't note everything found in every shop--we're just suggesting where to start searching. Happy hunting.

I appreciate your letters and phone calls and welcome your comments and suggestions.

Warm regards,

Irene Taylor

BAROQUE
SILVERSMITH, INC.

Expert Silversmith • Since 1965 • Trained in Europe

312-357-2813 • 847-677-7638

Sterling, Copper, Brass,
Pewter & Silverplate
Repair, Polish, Expert
Gold Plating

Lamps & Chandeliers
wired and refinished
Sterling Silverware
Repaired

Brass Bed repaired,
polished & lacquered

Costume & Antique
Jewelry, Fireplace, Door
& Plumbing Hardware
Polished & Plated

All work done on
Permises

Free Estimates
Free Pick-up & Delivery
City & Suburbs

Baroque Silversmith
5 N. Wabash #400
Chicago, IL 60602

SANDWICH ANTIQUES MARKET

SANDWICH, ILLINOIS
The Fairgrounds — U.S. 34

SUNDAYS
1997

May 18   Jun 22   Jul 27
Aug 17   Sep 28   Oct 26

8:00 a.m. to 4:00 p.m.
Rain or Shine

OUR 10TH ANNIVERSARY

FOOD * FREE PARKING * NO PETS
Admission $4.00 Per Person

Over 500 Quality Exhibitors
All Merchandise Guaranteed
Furniture Delivery Service Available

(773) 227-4464
http://www.antiquemarkets.com

Contents

Where you'll find the kicky old stuff,
antiques, elegancies and prime junk.

ILLINOIS

❦

WISCONSIN 149

For inquiries about shop listings, display advertising or discount
schedules, contact: Moonlight Press, 202 N. Brighton Place,
Arlington Heights, Illinois 60004, phone (847) 392-8438.

Towns & Cities

(continued)

Towns & Cities *(continued)*

ILLINOIS (continued)

Oak Park	215
Oregon	143
Orland Park	227
Oswego	208
Palatine	118
Park Ridge	113
Pearl City	144
Pecatonica	142
Plainfield	207
Plano	209
Prairie View	99
Richmond	131
Ridgefield	127
Riverside	218
Rockford	139
Rockton	142
Sandwich	209
Savanna	146
Schaumburg	117
Skokie	69
Somonauk	211
St. Charles	191
Steger	233
Sterling	145
Stockton	142
Stillman Valley	143
Sycamore	199
Union	122
Villa Park	186
Volo	107
Warren	142
Warrenville	207
Waterman	213
Wauconda	105
Waukegan	91
Westmont	204
Wheaton	191
Wheeling	97
Willow Springs	221
Wilmette	69
Wilmington	241
Winnetka	79
Woodstock	125
Yorkville	210
Zion	95

WISCONSIN

Afton	180
Beloit	177
Bristol	156
Brodhead	178
Brookfield	161
Browntown	179
Burlington	176
Caledonia	156
Cambridge	182
Cedarburg	166
Clinton	176
Columbus	183
Deerfield	182
Delafield	163
Delavan	173
Edgerton	181
Elkhorn	172
Fort Atkinson	182
Germantown	166
Grafton	168
Hartland	164
Janesville	180
Kenosha	149
Lake Geneva	171
Lake Mills	182
Lannon	165
Menomonee Falls	166
Merton	166
Milton	180
Milwaukee	157
Monroe	178
Oconomowoc	164
Pewaukee	164
Port Washington	170
Racine	155
Rubicon	170
Springfield	172
Sturtevant	152
Sussex	165
Union Grove	157
Walworth	174
Waterford	177
Waukesha	162
Wauwatosa	161
West Allis	161
West Milwaukee	161
Williams Bay	174
Wilmot	170

IOWA

Maquoketa	146

15

16

17

18

"Hard-to-Find"
Repair People, Services & Replacement Parts
Index

Copper
  Plating, 2,,9,12,16/17
  Repair, restore, polish, 2,9,12,
    16/17
  Re-tin cookware, 2,9,16/17
Costume rental, 61
Crystal repair, 70,269
Cybis restoration, 86

D

Danish cord, 84
Decorating Service, 90
Depression glass matching, 98,115
Dolls,
  Repair & restore, 210
Doors, antique, 29,55,206
Door hardware, polished & plated,
  2,9,12,16/17
    Installation, 67
    Restoration, 67
    Retrofitting, 67

E

Estate Auctions, 37,39,104
Estate liquidations, 39,58,121
Estate & House Sales Conducted,
  61,98,104,107,115,155,186,187
  202,212,216,222
    Partial households, 187
    Pricing, 187
Estate planning insurance appraisal,
  31,86
European buying tour, 45

F

Finders service, 35,67,68,188
Fireplace implements repaired, 12
Fireplace mantels,55,104,206,216
  Victorian tile sets, 216
Flea Markets/Antique Mkts, 10,18,
  23,108,136,147,159,202,248,
  250,256
Floral arrangements, 96,116
Floral custom designs, 96
Florida Guide, 15
Fostoria glass matching, 73,98
Foundry service, 216
Framing, picture, restoration, 90
Fretwork, 55
Furniture
  Carving repair, 28,66,90,148
  Custom design, 28,224
  French polish, 28,148
  In home touch-up, 66
  Inlay repair, 28,66,148
  Original finish conservation, 28,148
  Parts duplicated, 28,66
  Polishing, 28,66
  Refinishing supplies, 55,176,194
  Restoration, repair, refinish, 28,
    66,93,95,98,130,148,206,209,233
  Small furniture restoration, 66,90
  Stripping, 206
  Veneer repair, 28,66,148

G

Garden furniture & ornaments,35,38
Gas welding,12
Gemologist, 116
Gift certificates, 71

Glass
  Beveling, custom, 206
  Chips, polished, 12,269
  Cut glass repair, 269
  Cutting, custom, 269
  Design, custom, 269
  Engraving, custom, 269
  Repair, 70,209,269
  Stained & leaded repair, 95
Glassware pattern matching, 73,98
Gold
  Jewelry repair, 9,89
  Plating, 2,9,12,16/17
  Repair & restore, 2,,9,12,16/17
Goldsmith, 2,9,12,16/17
Guides to antique shops, 228

H

Hardware, 2,12,16/17,29,55,206,216
  Door, installation, 67
  Duplication, 216
  Polished, plated, repair,
    2,9,12,67,216
  Restoration, 67
  Retrofitting, 67
Heisey glass matching, 73,98
House sales conducted (see Estate
  sales)
Hummel restoration, 86,90

I

Identify antiques, 86
Illinois Guide to Shops, 200
Inlay repair, 28,66
Insurance appraisers, 31,86
  (also see Appraisers)
Internet, 30,42,68
Iowa Guide to shops, 244
Iron (wrought) repair, 2,12,16/17
Ivory repair, 90

J

Jewelry
  Appraisals, 112,197,211
  Costume, polished & plated, 9
  Custom design, 197
  Polished & plated, 9
  Repair & restore, 9,89,112,188,
    197,211
  Watch repair, 89,188,197,209

L

Lacquering metal, 2,12,206
Lamps
  Chimneys, shades, 137
  Made from your object, 2,9,12,16/17
  Parts, old & new, 2,12,16/17,137
  Polishing, 2,,9,12,16/17,137
  Repair & rewire,2,9,12,16/17,
    137,216,222
Lecturers, 68,196,212
Lighting fixtures
  Custom design, 2,9,16/17
  Interior & exterior, 12,55
  Repair, rewire & restore, 2,9,
    16/17,216
Lionel train repair, 211
Lladro restoration, 86,90
Locksmith, 16/17

M

Malls of USA Guide, 245
Mantels, 55,104,206,216,224
Marquetry repair, 148
Matching Services, 70,73,98
Matching service, China, 70,73,115
    Glassware, 73,98
    Silverplate, 70,73
Metal
    Plating, polish, laquer, 2,9,12,
      16/17,209
    Stripping, 2,9,12,16/17
Mirror resilvering, 9,209
Moulding, old, 55,206
    Repro, 55
Moving sales, 187
Museums, 106,110,160
Music box repair, 114,216,222

N

Necklace restringing, 89,197
Nickelodeons, repair & restore, 198

O

Oriental antiques appraised, 86,117,214
      Restored, 86,90
Organs, pump, restored, 198,214

P

Pewter, repair & restore, 2,9,12,16/17
Phonographs, antique repair,
    9,214,216,222
      Needles, 214
      Metal horn restoration, 9,214,216
      Picture Frame restoration, 90
Pinball machines, 207
Plating, 2,,9,12,16/17,216
Player Piano, rebuild/repair, 198,214
    Rolls for sale, 214
Pocket watch repair, 89,114
    Appraisals, 89
Polishing metal, 2,,9,12,16/17,216
Porcelain/Pottery repair & restoration,
    70,86,90
Pot metal repair, 9,12
Press releases written, 212
Pricing household goods, 187
Programs for groups, 68,196,212
Prop rental, 39,58,61
Publications, 15,23,167,200,212,
    239,244,245,256

R

Rattan repair, 84
Reference books, 163
Refinishing supplies, 55,176,194,206
Rentals, prop, 4,39,58,61
Repair, restore, refinish furniture
    (see Furniture)
Research consultant, 4,67,84
Resilver mirrors, 9,209
Restaurants, 118,144,145,232,240
Re-tin copper cookware, 2,9
Restoration service, 90
Royal Doulton restoration, 86
Rush work, 84,107,243

S

Salvage research service, 67
Search for antiques, 35,67,68,188
Ship model restoration, 90
Shows, antique, 10,18,246,
    248,250,256
Silk flower arrangements, 96,116
Silver, sterling
    Flatware repaired, 9,16/17
    Jewelry repair, 9,188
    Matching service, 70,73
    Plating, 2,9,12,16/17
    Repair & restore, 2,9,12,16/17,26
    Search service, 73
Silverplate flatware matching, 73
Silversmith, 2,9,16/17
Speakers, 68,196,212
Spelter repair, 9,12,16/17
Stained glass windows, 29,55,95
    134,206
      Repair & restoration, 95,206
      120,204
Sterling (see Silver)
Stripping furniture, 130,206
    Metal, 2,9,12,16/17
    Supplies, 206

T

Telephone repair, 222
Tin
    Ceilings, 55
    Repair, 2,9,16/17
    Re-tin copper cookware, 2,9,16/17
Tours conducted, 45,234
Toy repair, 211
Trade antiques, 101
Trains, electric, repair, 211
    Accessories repaired, 211
Trunk hardware, 206
    Duplication, 216

U

Upholstery, 28,66

V

Veneer repaired, 28,66,148
Videos (see page 72 for complete list)
    Queen Anne Chairs, 72
    Pressed Glass, 72
    Lalique, 72
    Norwegian Antiques, 72
    Prints, 72
    Haviland China, 72
    Scent bottles, 72
    Toys, 72

W

Watch repair, 89,114,188,209
    Pocket watch repair, 89,114
    Modern watch repair, 114
Web Sites, 30,42,68
White metal repair, 9,12,16/17
Wholesale to the trade, 61,
Wicker repair & restoration, 71,243
    Baby buggy restoration, 233
Wood carving repair, 28,66,90,148
Wood repair (see furniture)
World Wide Web, 30,42,68

HOW TO USE THIS GUIDE

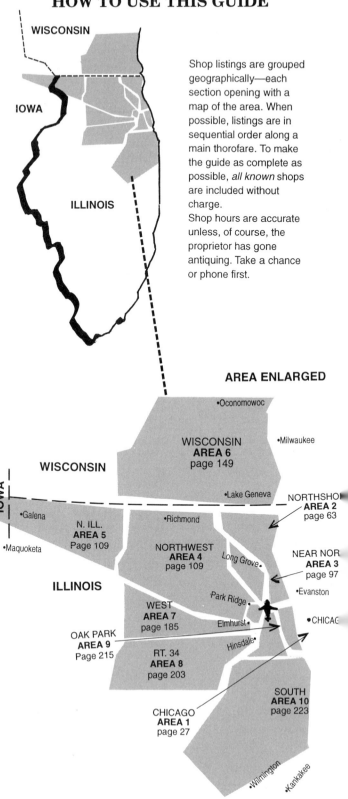

WISCONSIN

IOWA

ILLINOIS

Shop listings are grouped geographically—each section opening with a map of the area. When possible, listings are in sequential order along a main thorofare. To make the guide as complete as possible, *all known* shops are included without charge.

Shop hours are accurate unless, of course, the proprietor has gone antiquing. Take a chance or phone first.

AREA ENLARGED

•Oconomowoc

WISCONSIN
AREA 6
page 149

•Milwaukee

WISCONSIN

IOWA

•Galena

•Maquoketa

N. ILL.
AREA 5
Page 109

•Lake Geneva

NORTHSHO
AREA 2
page 63

•Richmond

NORTHWEST
AREA 4
page 109

Long Grove.

NEAR NOR
AREA 3
page 97

•Evanston

Park Ridge .

ILLINOIS

WEST
AREA 7
page 185

Elmhurst•

• CHICAG

OAK PARK
AREA 9
Page 215

Hinsdale•

RT. 34
AREA 8
page 203

SOUTH
AREA 10
page 223

CHICAGO
AREA 1
page 27

•Wilmington

•Kankakee

22

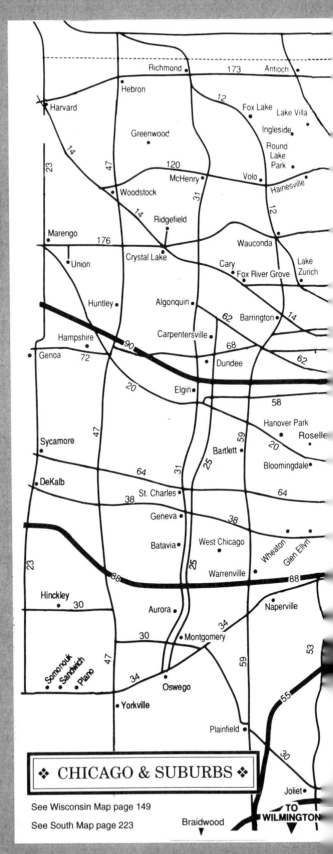

❖ CHICAGO & SUBURBS ❖

See Wisconsin Map page 149
See South Map page 223

24

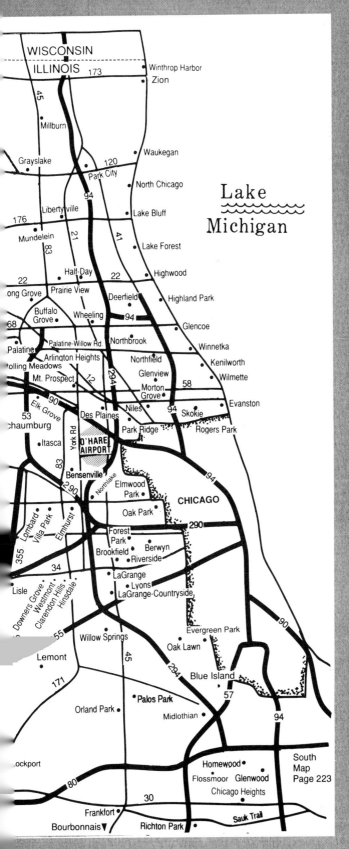

WISCONSIN
ILLINOIS 173
Winthrop Harbor
Zion

45

Millburn

Grayslake
120
Park City

Waukegan

North Chicago

94

176
Libertyville
Lake Bluff

21

Lake Michigan

Mundelein
83

41

Lake Forest

22
Half-Day
22
Highwood

ong Grove Prairie View
Deerfield
Highland Park

Buffalo
Grove
Wheeling
94

68

Palatine-Willow Rd. Northbrook
Glencoe

Palatine
Arlington Heights
Winnetka

olling Meadows
Northfield
Kenilworth

Mt. Prospect
12
294
Glenview
58
Wilmette

90
Elk Grove
Morton
Grove

53
Des Plaines
Niles
94
Skokie

chaumburg
Park Ridge
Rogers Park

Itasca

York Rd.

O'HARE
AIRPORT

Evanston

83

Bensenville
Northlake

94

2.90
Elmwood
Park
CHICAGO

Lombard
Villa Park
Elmhurst
Oak Park

355
Forest
Park
290

34
Brookfield
Berwyn
Riverside

Lisle
LaGrange
Lyons
LaGrange-Countryside

Downers Grove
Westmont
Clarendon Hills
Hinsdale

90

55
Willow Springs
Evergreen Park

Lemont
Oak Lawn

45

171
294
Blue Island

Orland Park
Palos Park
57

Midlothian
94

ockport

Homewood
South
Map
Page 223

80
Flossmoor Glenwood
Chicago Heights

30

Frankfort

Bourbonnais
Richton Park
Sauk Trail

26

Area 1
CHICAGO

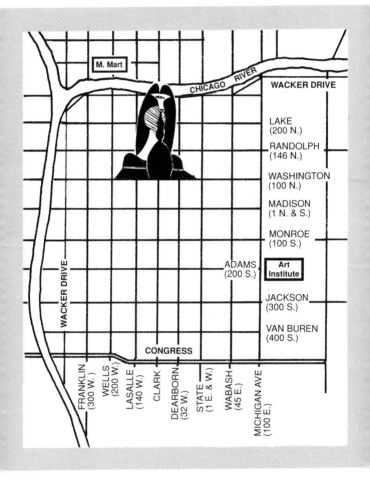

Downtown

Poster Plus
200 S. Michigan Ave.
Phone (312) 461-9277
Mon. thru Fri. 10 to 6, Sat. 9:30 to 6, Sun. 11 to 6.
Vintage posters-prior to 1950. Turn-of-the-century French and American, travel, World War I & II.

Antiques on the Avenue
104 S. Michigan Ave. (corner of Monroe, 2nd floor)
Phone (312) 357-2800
Mon. thru Fri. 10 to 7, Sat. & Sun. 11 to 5.
They moved a little bit south of their former location. Many fine dealers are represented here. including:

> **Silver Treasures,** *Sterling silver - Antique American, English and continental.*

GALLERIA 733

Custom Louis XV/Normandy Style Entertainment Center, Cherry

WORKSHOP

Specializing in high quality, handcrafted
and carved custom pieces made to
specification.
Complete repair, restoration, refinishing
and upholstery facilities by skilled
Master European Craftsmen -
on premises.

SHOWROOM • TO THE TRADE ONLY

Featuring one of Chicago's finest collections
of Country French, Period and Art Deco
Furnishings and Accessories from the
18th, 19th and 20th century.

Come visit our new showroom & workshop:

GALLERIA 733
733 W. Lake Street (at Halsted)
Chicago, Illinois 60606
(312) 382-0546
(312) 382-0548 Fax

Monday - Friday 9:00 to 5:00 • Saturday 10:00 to 3:00
Also by appointment

CHICAGO / Downtown *(continued)*

Beaux Arts Gallery
106 S. Michigan Ave.
Phone (312) 444-1991
Monday thru Saturday 10:30 to 5:30.
Bronzes, marble statuary, paintings, academic drawings. medallic art, art pottery.

Costume Jewelry Repair House
10 N. Michigan
Phone (312) 782-7810
Monday thru Friday 10 to 6, Sat. 10 to 3.
Antique, vintage and costume jewelry.

Carteaux Inc. Jewelers
31 N. Wabash Ave.
Phone (312) 782-5375
Mon. thru Fri. 10 to 5:30, Thurs. 'til 6:30, Sat. 10 to 5.
Fine antique jewelry: Victorian, Art Deco, Art Nouveau. Also new jewelry.

Marshall Field's
Caledonian Antiques Gallery
111 N. State St.
Phone (312) 781-5713
Mon. thru Sat. 9:45 to 5:45, Mon. & Thurs. 'til 7.
On the 8th floor facing Wabash Ave. is the Gallery with English & French furniture & accessories, also reproductions.

Harlan J. Berk Ltd.
31 N. Clark St.
Phone (312) 609-0016
Monday thru Friday 9 to 4:45.
We're talking real antiques- 4000 BC to 1453 AD. You can see authentic classical museum pieces up close - not behind glass. Small ancient items can be purchased for as little as $10.

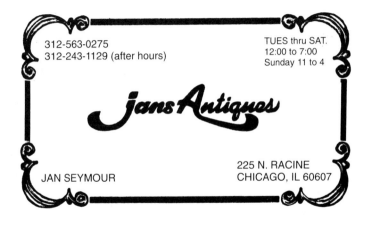

CHICAGO / Downtown *(continued)*

Galleria 733
733 W. Lake Street (at Halsted St. 800 W.)
Phone (312) 382-0546
Monday thru Friday 9 to 5, Sat. 10 to 3.
A complete repair and custom design workshop.
Also a showroom of country French, period and
art deco furnishings to the trade. All on one floor.

Jan's Antiques
225 N. Racine (1200 W.)
Phone (312) 563-0275
Tuesday thru Saturday 12:30 to 7, Sun. 11 to 4:30.
Two floors of architectural antiques—mantels,
doors, etc. Also clocks, lamps, desks. A good portion
of the furniture is sold "as is."

Salvage One
1524 South Sangamon St. (South of downtown)
Phone (312) 733-0098
Tuesday thru Saturday 10 to 5, Sun. 11 to 4.
5 floors of mantels, doors, tubs, hardware, etc.

Pilsen Gallery
540 W. 18th Street
Phone (312) 829-2827 & (312) 633-9038
Monday thru Saturday 11 to 7.
Architectural artifacts, antique furniture.

Merchandise Mart Plaza
At Wells St. and the Chicago River

The mart is a wholesale center for decorators and
architects. Some shops, but not all, will let you
browse in their showroom unaccompanied, but
any purchases must be made through your
decorator or architect.

Merchandise Mart *(continued)*

Richard Norton, Inc.
6th floor - 612
Phone (312) 644-9359
*18th & early 19th C. French & English antiques
and accessories.*

Antiques, Ltd.
16th floor - 1626
Phone (312) 644-6530
*An unusual collection of antiques, many of
carved wood, wrought iron. Southwestern
furniture, chandeliers, lighting.*

Richard Himmel Antique &
Decorative Furniture
18th floor - 1800
Phone (312) 527-5700
*17th, 18th 19th & 20th C. European & American
furniture and decorative arts.*

Mike Bell
18th floor - 1869
Phone (312) 644-6848
French & English country furniture.

CHICAGO

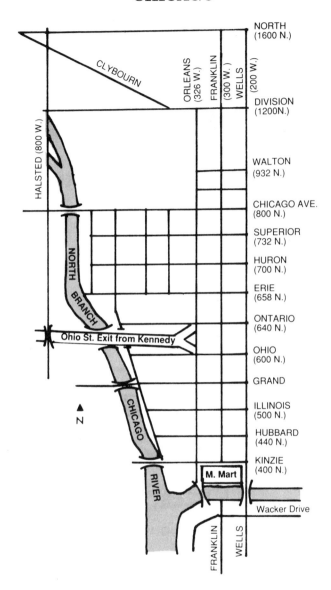

River North

The Antiquarians Bldg.
159 W. Kinzie St. (east of Wells St.)
Phone (312) 527-0533
Monday thru Saturday 10 to 6.
This shop on Kinzie offers antiques from 5
continents. There are 22 dealers including:

Oriental Treasures
Chinese & Japanese Antiques

Silver Treasures • *Sterling silver - Antique*
American, English and Continental

CHICAGO / River North *(continued)*

Jay Robert's Antique Warehouse Inc.
149 W. Kinzie St.
Phone (312) 222-0167
Monday thru Saturday 10 to 5.
Welsh dressers, beds, etc. on the 1st floor. Up a steep
flight to more furniture, fireplace mantels, etc.

The Antiques Centre
220 W. Kinzie (west of Wells St.)
Phone (312) 464-1946
Monday thru Friday 10 to 5, Sat. 12 to 4.
A gathering of fine antique dealers
offering everything from 18th C. furniture to folk art.

Tompkins & Robandt
220 W. Kinzie - 4th floor
Phone (312) 645-9995
Monday thru Friday 11 to 5.
One of a kind antiques. Decorative continental
furnishings and accessories.

Milvia Swan Antiques
406 N. Wells St.
Phone (312) 527-4446
Monday thru Friday 11 to 6.
Prints, continental accessories, furniture, lighting.

312.645-9995

TOMPKINS & ROBANDT
Antique and Decorative Continental Furnishings

220 W. Kinzie Street
4th floor

Chicago, Illinois 60610

CHICAGO / River North *(continued)*
Rita Bucheit, Ltd.
449 N. Wells St.
Phone (312) 527-4080
Monday thru Saturday 10 to 6.
*Empire and Biedermeier furnishings from the
first half of the 19th century.*

Sara Breiel Antiques
449 N. Wells St. (entrance on Illinois St.)
Phone (312) 923-9223
Monday thru Friday 11 to 5, Sat. 12 to 4.
*Antique English & continental furniture,
decorative accessories.*

Pimlico Antiques, Ltd.
500 N. Wells St.
Phone (312) 245-9199
Monday thru Friday 10 to 5, Sat. 11 to 5.
17th to 19th C. English & continental furniture.

Christa's Ltd.
217 W. Illinois St.
Phone (312) 222-2520
Monday thru Saturday 10 to 5.
*Fine furniture and accessories. Not your
typical River North shop. What fun. Everything
piled high, mirrors hanging from the rafters.*

Leslie Hindman Auctioneers
215 W. Ohio St.
Phone (312) 670-0010
*Auctions of furniture, decorations, silver,
jewelry, 19th & 20th C. paintings and prints.*

Gallery 1945
225 W. Huron St.
Phone (312) 573-1945
Wednesday thru Saturday 12 to 5.

CHICAGO / River North *(continued)*

Portals, Ltd.
230 W. Huron
Phone (312) 642-1066
Tuesday thru Friday 9:30 to 4:30, Sat. 11 to 4.
*19th C. furniture & decorative objects, sophisti-
cated naif paintings by international artists.*

Taskey's Antiques
230 W. Huron St., 2-E
Phone (312) 944-7128
Monday thru Friday 11 to 4, To The Trade Only.
*17th, 18th, early 19th C. English, continental
and American antiques.*

Dunning's Auction Service
325 W. Huron St., Suite 408
Phone (312) 664-8400
*Chicago office of the 100-year old
Elgin based company.*

Robert Henry Adams Fine Art
715 N. Franklin
Phone (312) 642-8700
Tuesday thru Friday 10 to 5, Sat. 12 to 5.
*American regionalist and modern paintings,
prints and sculpture.*

CHICAGO / River North *(continued)*

Mongerson Wunderlich Gallery
702 N. Wells St.
Phone (312) 943-2354
Tuesday thru Saturday 9:30 to 5:30.
American western paintings and prints.

O'Hara's Gallery
707 N. Wells St.
Phone (312) 751-1286
Monday thru Saturday 10 to 5.
From ornate continental pieces to a
Revere style bowl.

Fly-By-Nite Gallery
714 N. Wells
Phone (312) 664-8136 or (312) 337-0264
Monday thru Saturday 12 to 5, appt. suggested.
Everything is labeled, almost like a museum.
Unusual European and American art pottery
and other art objects.

Schwebel
311 W. Superior St.
Phone (312) 280-1998
Monday thru Friday 10 to 5, Sat. 12 to 5.
19th C. American furniture and accessories.

Michael Fitzsimmon's Decorative Arts
311 W. Superior St., 1st floor
Phone (312) 787-0496
Tues. thru Fri. 10 to 6, Sat. 11 to 5.
American Arts & Crafts: furniture, lighting,
ceramics, accessories.

Old Vienna Antiques
1543 N. Wells St.
Phone (312) 335-9354
Tuesday thru Saturday 11 to 6.
Biedermeier and Empire furniture.

Vintage Posters International
1551 N. Wells St.
Phone (312) 951-6681
Mon. thru Fri. 11 to 7, Sat. 'til 6, Sun. 12 to 5.
American and European posters 1880-1950.
Antiques, costume and vintage jewelry.

Pine & Design Imports
511 W. North Ave.
Phone (312) 640-0100
Mon. thru Sat. 10 to 6, Mon. & Thurs. 'til 8,
Sunday 12 to 5.
European antique pine furniture.

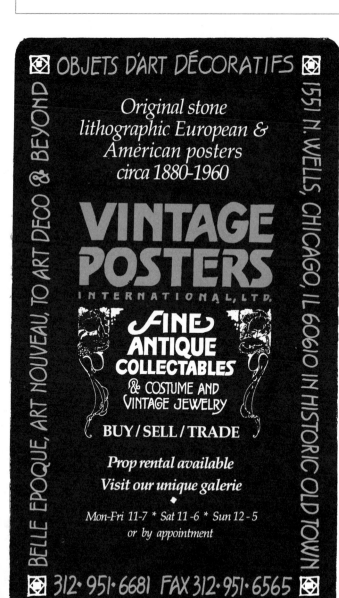
39

CHICAGO

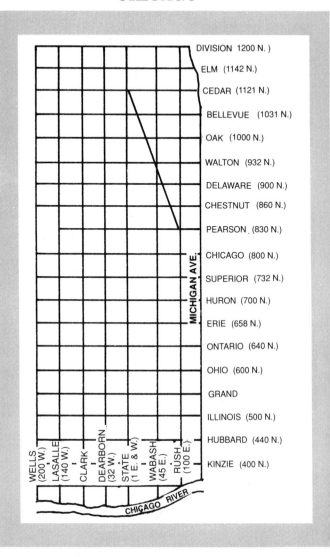

North Michigan Ave. (and west to Wells St.)

Golden Triangle
72 W. Hubbard St.
Phone (312) 755-1266
Monday thru Friday 10 to 7, Sat. 10 to 5.
Antique Chinese country furniture & antique British Colonial furniture from Burma.

CHICAGO / North Michigan Ave. *(cont.)*

Tree Studio
613 N. State St
Phone (312) 337-7541
Mon. 12 to 6, Tues. thru Sat. 11 to 6.
*Turn of the century to the 60s. Specializing
in Art Deco and American Art. The Tree Studio, built
in 1894, was Chicago's first building designed
specifically as affordable studios for artists.*

Cathay Gallery
620 N. Michigan Ave.
Phone (312) 951-1048

The Decro Gallery
224 E. Ontario-1st floor (east of Michigan Ave.)
Phone (312) 943-4847
Monday thru Saturday 10:30 to 5:30.
*Antique furniture and accessories from Japan,
China and Korea.*

Saito Oriental Antiques Inc.
645 N. Michigan Ave., Suite 428
Phone (312) 642-4366
Monday thru Friday 10:30 to 5:30, Sat. 11 to 5,
appointment suggested.
Chinese, Japanese and Korean antiques.

Studio V
672 N. Dearborn
Phone (312) 440-1937
Monday thru Saturday 12 to 6.
*Thousands of pieces of costume jewelry, art deco
artifacts, cobalt blue glass, antique telephones.*

Johnson Antiques, Ltd.
172 E. Walton Pl.
Phone (312) 440-9466
Tuesday thru Saturday 10 to 5.
*18th & 19th C. fine jewelry and objects of art,
antique silver.*

Malcolm Franklin, Inc.
34 E. Oak St.
Phone (312) 337-0202
Monday thru Friday 9 to 5, Sat. 9 to 3.
Antiques and furniture from England.

***Index to
"Hard-to-Find" Repair People,
Services and Replacement Parts
page 19.***

CHICAGO

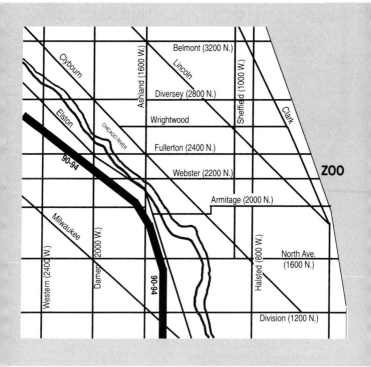

Lincoln Park Area & West

Exposa Inc.
230 W. North Ave. in Pipers Alley
Phone (312) 944-8454
Call for hours.
Fine Biedermeier furniture.

Green Acres
1464 N. Milwaukee Ave.
Phone (773) 292-1998
Tuesday thru Sunday 12 to 6.
Victorian, Empire, Arts & Crafts antique home furnishings.

U.S. #1 Antiques
1509 N. Milwaukee Ave.
Phone (773) 489-9428
Wednesday thru Sunday 12 to 6.
Victorian, Art Nouveau, Deco.

Modern Times
1538 N. Milwaukee Ave.
Phone (773) 772-8871
Wed. thru Fri. 1 to 6, Sat. Sun. 12 to 6.
Furnishings from art deco to disco.

CHICAGO / Lincoln Park *(continued)*

Zigurat Architectural Ornament
1702 N. Milwaukee Ave.
Phone (773) 227-6290
7 days, 11 to 6.
Stained & art glass, vintage garden ornaments, period lighting, architectural antiques and more.

Portia Gallery
1702 N. Damen
Phone (773) 862-1700
Tues. thru Fri. 12 to 7, Sat. 'til 5, Sun. 12 to 4.
All glass - contemporary and antique.

Armitage Antique Gallery
1529 W. Armitage (West of the Chicago River, just off Elston Ave.)
Phone (773) 227-7727
7 days, 11 to 6.
Every mall has it's own personality because of the blend of dealers—you'll find everything from fine pottery and silver jewelry to radios and some wonderful funky stuff.

Reflections Antiques
2156 N. Clybourn Ave.
Phone (773) 871-7078
Mon. thru Fri. 11 to 7, Sat. & Sun. 10 to 6.
Lighting and furniture, 1820 to 1920.

An Antique Store
1450 W. Webster
Phone (312) 935-6060
Monday thru Friday 11 to 7, Sat. Sun 10 to 6.
Art Deco, moderne, Heywood-Wakefied, 50's furniture & smalls.

Ile de France Antiques
2222 N. Elston Ave.
Phone (773) 227-0704
Monday thru Saturday 10 to 6.
French furniture & accessories.

CHICAGO / Lincoln Park *(continued)*

Russ's Pier W
1227 W. Diversey Pky.
Phone (773) 327-5718
Open 7 days (includes most Tuesdays.)

Aged Experience Antiques, etc.
2034 N. Halsted St.
Phone (773) 975-9790
Tuesday thru Saturday 12 to 6, Sun. 'til 5.
Very country.

Turtle Creek Antiques
850 W. Armitage Ave.
Phone (773) 327-2630
Tues. thru Sat. 12 to 6, Sun. 12 to 5.
Quilts, textiles, jewelry, country furniture, smalls.

Stanley Galleries
2118 N. Clark St.
Phone (773) 281-1614
Monday thru Saturday 12 to 7.
Restored American antique light fixtures.

CHICAGO

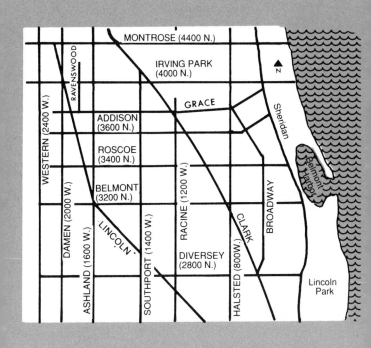

Lake View area

International Antiques
2300 W. Diversey
Phone (773) 227-2400
Open 7 days, 11 to 6.
*Jack and Pam have renovated the former
warehouse into an indoor village square bordered
with individual shops. Dealers with antiques from
around the world.*

Chicago Riverfront Antique Mart
2929 N. Western Ave.
Phone (773) 252-2500
Monday thru Saturday 10 to 6, Sun. 12 to 6.
*Antique dealers, repairs and shows have
transformed the Hammond Organ factory into
a 3-story complex.*

North Lincoln Avenue (and vicinity):

Steve Starr Studios
2779 N. Lincoln Ave.
Phone (773) 525-6530
Monday thru Friday 2 to 6, Sat. Sun. 1 to 5.
*Art Deco and moderne furnishings and accessories,
costume jewelry, specializing in picture frames.
He wrote the book on deco photo frames,
Picture Perfect.*

Time Well Consignment
2780 N. Lincoln Ave.
Phone (773) 549-2113
6 days: Wed. & Thurs. 11 to 8, Fri. thru
Mon. 11 to 5, closed Tuesday.
Depression era, new and antique furniture.

Wallner Antiques
1229 W. Diversey
Phone (773) 248-6061
Monday thru Saturday 11 to 6, Sun. 12 to 5.
Furniture including French & Italian,
accessories, tapestries, paintings, etc.

Powell's Book Store
2850 N. Lincoln Ave.
Phone (773) 248-1444
7 days: Sun. thru Fri. 11 to 9, Sat. 10 to 10.
Out of print, rare and used books.

Gallery Bernard
2902 N. Lincoln Ave.
Phone (773) 248-9363
Mon. thru Fri. 11 to 6, Sat. & Sun. 12 to 6.
Antiques, fine decorative furniture, accessories.

Urban Artifacts
2928 N. Lincoln Ave.
Phone (773) 404-1008
Wednesday thru Sunday 1 to 6.
Good design is always in style. Vintage modern
furniture and decorative arts circa 1940s to 1970s.

Collectibles Etc. Etc.
3012 N. Lincoln Ave.
Phone (773) 348-1101
7 days 12 to 6.
Collectibles, antiques, silversmith.

Chicago Antique Centre
3045 N. Lincoln Ave.
Phone (773) 929-0200
7 days, 11 to 6.
From antique maps to rhinestone jewelry.

Red Eye Antiques
3050 N. Lincoln Ave.
Phone (773) 975-2020
Saturday & Sunday 12 to 6.
Art Deco, architectural, folk art, jewelry, pottery.

Harlon's Antiques
3058 N. Lincoln Ave.
Phone (773) 327-3407
Mon. 10:30 to 2, Tues. thru Sun. 10:30 to 4:30.
Lamps, paintings, prints, jewelry.

CHICAGO / Lake View *(continued)*

Wacky Cats
3109 N. Lincoln Ave.
Phone (773) 929-6701
Monday thru Friday 12 to 7, Sat. 12 to 6,
Sunday 12 to 5.
Vintage clothing, shoes, hats, some men's clothing.
From Victorian to funky 70s.

Lincoln Antique Mall
3141 N. Lincoln Ave.
Phone (773) 244-1440
7 days, 11 to 7.
A new mall in this area.

ZigZag
3419 N. Lincoln Ave.
Phone (773) 525-1060
Wednesday thru Friday 2 to 6, Sat. 1 to 6,
Sunday 1 to 4.
Marsha's shop has 20th C. furnishings, objects
and jewelry, emphasing industrial design &
metalwork. Large selection of unique Bakelite
jewelry & objects. Costume jewelry, plastic
purses, radios, lighting.

Lake View Antiques
3422 N. Lincoln Ave.
Phone (773) 935-6443
Wednesday thru Saturday 11 to 5, Sun. 12 to 4.
Quality china, linens, furniture, silver.

Carousel Upscale Resale & Antiques
3511 N. Lincoln Ave.
Phone (773) 868-4888
Monday thru Saturday 11 to 6, Sun. 12 to 5.
Resale, antiques, collectibles.

One More Time
3526 N. Lincoln Ave.
Phone (773) 868-1498
Wed. thru Fri. 10 to 8, Sat. 10 to 6, Sun. 12 to 5.

Daniels Antiques
3711 N. Ashland
Phone (773) 868-9355
Wednesday thru Saturday 11 to 6, Sun. 12 to 5.
*Eclectic furnishings, art and architectural
items from all periods.*

Extra Fancy
3827 N. Lincoln Ave.
Phone (773) 665-2367
Wednesday thru Friday 2 to 7, Sat. Sun. 12 to 6.
*Specializing in bar and smoking paraphernalia,
American dinnerware.*

Jazz'e Junque Shop
3831 N. Lincoln
Phone (773) 472-1500
Tues. Thurs. 12 to 5:30, Wed. call for hours,
Fri. 12 to 6:30, Sat. 10:30 to 4:30,
open Sundays during Christmas.
*If you're looking for cookie jars, this is the place.
1,500 are on display. Also kitchen collectibles,
salt & peppers, etc.*

Lincoln Avenue Antique Co-Op
3851 N. Lincoln Ave.
Phone (773) 935-6600
Wednesday thru Sunday 12 to 6.
They cover every era and all price ranges.

Magpie
3851 N. Lincoln Ave.
Same address and hours as above.

Kelmscott Gallery
4611 N. Lincoln
Phone (773) 784-2559
Tuesday thru Saturday 11 to 6.
*Decorative arts. Specializing in Frank
Lloyd Wright furniture.*

CHICAGO / Lake View *(continued)*

Belmont Avenue:

Weisz Antique Resources
1741 W. Belmont Ave.
Phone (773) 871-4242
Tuesday thru Saturday 11 to 5.
18th C. thru Deco. Paintings, prints, accessories, chandeliers.

Miscellania
1800 W. Belmont Ave.
Phone (773) 348-9647
Wednesday thru Sunday 12 to 5.
Long, narrow shop on the corner filled to the brim with Victorian to deco antiques.

Carlin Antiques
1819 W. Belmont Ave.
Phone (773) 549-7600
Wednesday thru Sunday 12 to 5.
Formal French & English furniture, lighting.

Ray's Antiques & Collectibles
1821 W. Belmont
Phone (773) 348-5150
Wednesday thru Saturday 12 to 6, Sun. 12 to 4.
Glass and furniture.

Antique House
1832 W. Belmont
Phone (773) 327-0707
Wednesday & Saturday & Sunday 1 to 5.
Furniture.

Antiques by S. F. Johnson
1901 W. Belmont Ave.
Phone (773) 477-9243
Wednesday thru Sunday 12 to 5.
40s and back. Primitives, Mission & Eastlake furniture and a variety of antiques.

20th Century Revue
1903 W. Belmont
Phone (773) 472-8890
Wednesday thru Sunday 12 to 5, Fri. Sat. 'til 6.
20s thru 50s furniture, fabrics, kitchen items, posters, lamps, accessories.

Nineteen Thirteen
1913 W. Belmont Ave.
Phone (773) 404-9522
Wednesday thru Sunday 12 to 5.
Eclectic mix of furniture, ethnic objects,

Kristina Maria Antiques
1919 W. Belmont Ave.
Phone (773) 472-2445
Saturday and Sunday 12 to 5.
French mahogany, carved furniture.

Belmont Antique Mall
2039 W. Belmont Ave.
Phone (773) 549-9270
7 days, 11 to 6.
45 dealers.

Phil's Factory Antique Mall
2040 W. Belmont Ave.
Phone (773) 528-8549
7 days, 11 to 6.
20 dealers.

House of Nostalgia
2047 W. Belmont Ave.
Phone (773) 244-6460
7 days 11:30 to 6:30.
Three floors of antiques including Royal Doulton, furniture, jewelry. 50s & 60s.

Caroline's Collectibles
2106 W. Belmont Ave.
Phone (773) 472-3434
Wednesday thru Sunday 12 to 5.
Furniture, glassware, kitchen collectibles, costume jewelry.

Father Time Antiques
2108 W. Belmont Ave.
Phone (773) 880-5599
Wednesday thru Sunday 12 to 5.
Wristwatches, clocks, imported furniture.

The Cracker Barrel Antiques
2120 W. Belmont
Phone (773) 296-2030
Open afternoons.

CHICAGO / Lake View *(continued)*

Collectique
2127 W. Belmont Ave.
Phone (773) 525-2300
Saturday & Sunday 12 to 5.
Cut glass, decorative accessories, linens, jewelry.

Danger City
2129 W. Belmont Ave.
Phone (773) 871-1420
7 days 11 to 6.
Yes, it's an antique shop. Unusual items of 20th C. The 3 owners from Milwaukee were cautioned so often about moving to Chicago—hence the name.

Sonia Simone
2132 W. Belmont Ave.
Phone (773) 296-0931
Fri. 1 to 5, Sat. 12 to 6, Sun. 12 to 5.
Linens, lace, hand painted porcelain, furniture, vintage clothing.

Carlos Antiques
2137 W. Belmont Ave.
Phone (773) 868-9140
Friday, Saturday, Sunday 11 to 5.
Specializing in radios, art deco, ocean liner memoribilia.

Good Old Days
2138 W. Belmont Ave.
Phone (773) 472-8837
Thursday thru Sunday 12 to 5.
American oak and walnut furniture, lamps, radios, neon beer signs.

CHICAGO / Lake View *(continued)*

James Furniture
2147 W. Belmont Ave.
Phone (773) 477-7745
Quality used furniture and fine antiques.

Belmont Antique Mall West
2229 W. Belmont Ave.
Phone (773) 871-3915
7 days 11 to 6.

Olde Chicago Antiques
2336-40 W. Belmont Ave.
Phone (773) 935-1200
Tuesday thru Saturday 11 to 5.
To the trade, past customers or make an appt.
French furniture, clocks, armoires.

North Clark Street (and vicinity):

Wild Thing
2933 N. Clark St.
Phone (773) 549-7787
Monday thru Saturday 12 to 7, Sun. 12 to 6.
*40s to the 70s men's & womens' vintage clothing
and accessories. Specializing in Bridal gowns.*

Look What I Found
2907 N. Broadway
Phone (773) 472-7202
Monday thru Friday 12 to 7, Sat. Sun. 10 to 7.
Collectibles, jewelry, vintage clothing, arts & crafts.

Past to Present
1109 W. Belmont (enter in back on Seminary St.)
Phone (773) 935-8181
Tuesday thru Sunday 12 to 7.
Furniture, costume jewelry, vintage clothing, lamps.

Wrigleyville Antique Mall
3336 N. Clark St.
Phone (773) 868-0285
Monday thru Saturday 11 to 6:30, Sun. 12 to 6.
*Bigger than ever— they now have 50 dealers
with American artifacts 1880 - 1960.*

Hubba-Hubba
3338 N. Clark St.
Phone (773) 477-1414
Monday thru Saturday 11 to 7, Sun. 12 to 5.
Vintage wedding apparel and new clothing.

Lake Shore Furniture
934 W. Roscoe (at Clark)
Phone (773) 327-0972
Monday thru Saturday 9 to 5.
Several floors of used furniture and antiques.

CHICAGO / Lake View *(continued)*

Strange Cargo
3448 N. Clark St.
Phone (773) 327-8090
Mon. thru Fri. 12 to 7, Sat. 11 to 7, Sun. 12 to 5.
Never worn vintage clothing.

Yesterdays
1143 W. Addison St
Phone (773) 248-8087
Monday thru Saturday 1 to 7, Sun. 2 to 6.
Political buttons, movie posters, magazines.

Renovation Source
3512 N. Southport
Phone (773) 327-1250
Tuesday thru Saturday 10 to 6.
Mantels, hardware, doors, moulding, fretwork, etc.
Everything for the renovator.

Wisteria
3715 N. Southport
Phone (773) 880-5868
Thurs. Fri. 4 to 9, Sat. 12 to 9, Sun. 12 to 5.
Vintage clothing for men, women & children.
Also collectibles.

Quake Collectibles
3759 N. Southport
Phone (773) 404-0607
Tuesday thru Friday 2 to 6, Sat. & Sun. 12 to 6.
60s and 70s toys.

North Broadway & Halsted Street:

Silver Moon
3337-3339 N. Halsted St.
Phone (773) 883-0222
Tuesday thru Sunday 12 to 6.
*Vintage clothing from the Victorian era to the
1960's for men and women. Also 19th & 20th C.
furniture and objects.*

Frock Shop
3402 N. Halsted St.
Phone (773) 871-2728
Tues. thru Fri. 1 to 8, Sat. 12 to 8, Sun. 1 to 6.
60s and 70s vintage funk.

Beatnix
3436 N. Halsted St.
Phone (773) 935-1188
Mon. thru Thurs. 12 to 9, Fri. 12 to 10, Sat. 11 to 10,
Sunday 12 to 8.
60's & 70's clothes, knick knacks.

Flashy Trash
3524 N. Halsted St.
Phone (773) 327-6900
Monday thru Saturday 11 to 8, Sun. 12 to 6.
*Vintage & contempory clothes, jewelry,
costumes for men & women.*

Americana
3924 N. Southport
Phone (773) 935-4204. By appointment.
Political buttons, paper Americana.

Architectural Artifacts, Inc.
4325 N. Ravenswood
Phone (773) 348-0622
7 days 10 to 5.
*Massive and small pieces of buildings—elevator
doors, tiles, mantels, light fixtures, etc.*

Evanstonia
4555 N. Ravenswood
Phone (773) 907-0101
Monday thru Saturday 11 to 6, Sun. 12 to 5.
*A huge combination showroom, workshop and
warehouse for furniture & accessories from 1850's
to 1940's. Complete dining and bedroom sets.
Their other shop, with the same name, is in Evanston.*

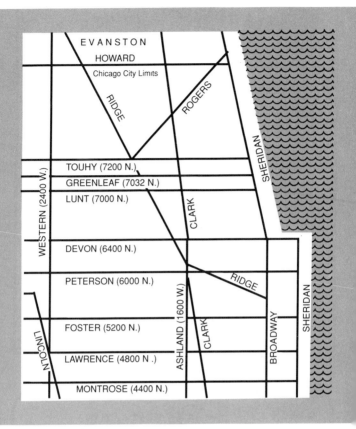

North Side/Rogers Park Area

Midwestern Arts & Antiques
4648 N. Western Ave.
Phone (773) 275-8210
Usually Mon. thru Sat. 11 to 6, best to call first.
Fine furniture, oriental rugs, jewelry, clocks.

Penn Dutchman
4912 N. Western Ave.
Phone (773) 271-2208
Monday thru Saturday 10 to 6, Sun. 12 to 5.
*11 rooms of wonderful odds and ends for
collectors, artists and fixer-uppers.*

Griffins & Gargoyles Ltd.
2140 W. Lawrence Ave.
Phone (773) 769-1255
Thurs. thru Mon. 11 to 6, closed Tues. & Wed.
*A two story charmer. Don't miss this one if you're
looking for European furniture— pine, armoires, etc.*

CHICAGO / North Side *(continued)*

Gibell's & Bits
5512 W. Lawrence Ave. (1/2 block east of Central)
Phone (773) 283-4065
Monday thru Saturday 11 to 5:30, Thurs. 'til 6:30.
Furniture, glassware, linens, costume jewelry.

Quality Antiques & Gifts
6401 N. Caldwell Ave.
Phone (773) 631-1134
5 days 11 to 4, closed Wed. & Sun.
Furniture, jewelry, glass.

ANDERSONVILLE
This is an area that has, in addition to the following antique shops, a Swedish restaurant, deli, bakery and a Swedish museum.

Really Heavy Antiques
5142 N. Clark St.
Phone (773) 784-7936
Wednesday thru Sunday 12 to 7.
Furniture and smalls, 40s to 70s.

The Acorn Antiques & Uniques, Ltd.
5241 N. Clark St.
Phone (773) 506-9100
Wed, thru Fri. 11 to 6, Sat. 10 to 6, Sun. 10 to 5.
A beautiful shop. See antique silver and crystal, exquisite boxes and glass and other treasures.

George's Antiques (Chicago's Recycle Shop)
5308 N. Clark St.
Phone (773) 878-8525
Monday thru Saturday 9 to 6.
Large second hand store.

Camden Passage Antique Market
5309 N. Clark St.
Phone (773) 989-0111
Tues. thru Fri. 11 to 7, Sat. 'til 6, Sun. 'til 4.
8 dealers.

Kyoto Traditions
1478 W. Catalpa Ave.
Phone (773) 275-2705
Saturday 11 to 5.

Fond Memories
6140 N. Clark St.
Phone (773) 764-1111
Fri. & Sat. 12 to 5, other days by chance.
Victorian antiques, collectibles, furniture, jewelry.

B. J. Furniture & Antiques
6901 N. Western Ave.
Phone (773) 262-1000
Monday thru Saturday 10 to 5.
5 showrooms of furniture.

Direct Auction Galleries
7232 N. Western Ave.
Phone (773) 465-3300
Auctions every 2 weeks, call them for details.

Richard's Antiques
7418 N. Western Ave.
Phone (773) 262-2004
Monday thru Saturday 9 to 3.
Quality furniture, oriental rugs, fine bric-a-brac.

Lost Eras Antiques & Lost Eras Costume Company
1509-19 W. Howard St.
Phone (773) 764-7400
Monday thru Saturday 10 to 6, Sun. 12 to 5.
Get all gussied up in vintage clothing - they have one of the largest selections in town (for men and women.) Also antiques from all periods.

61

Area 2
ALONG THE NORTH SHORE

In this section: Evanston, Morton Grove, Wilmette, Keniworth, Winnetka, Northfield, Glenview, Glencoe, Highland Park, Highwood, Lake Forest, Lake Bluff, Waukegan, West of Gurnee, Grayslake, Hainesville, Fox Lake, Antioch, Millburn, Zion.

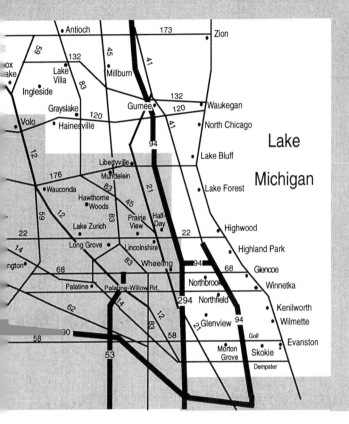

Evanston

Eureka! Antiques & Nostalgia & Collectibles
705 Washington St.
Phone (847) 869-9090
Tuesday thru Saturday 11 to 5.
Two floors of early tin, paper, advertising, clocks, deco, nostalgia. A fun shop.

Evanstonia Period Furniture & Restoration
702 Main St.
Phone (847) 869-0110
Monday thru Saturday 11 to 6, Sun. 12 to 5.
A shop full of furniture from 1850's to 1940's in beautiful condition. Gorgeous dining room sets.

EVANSTON *(continued)*

Rusty Nail Antiques
912 Sherman Ave.
Phone (847) 491-0360
Tuesday thru Saturday 11 to 5.
Cookbooks, lace by the yard, buttons, crochet work,
tablecloths, sewing machines, primitives.

B. J.'s Antiques
809 Main St.
Phone (847) 328-7590
Mon. thru Fri. 1 to 6, Sat. 10 to 6, Sun. 1 to 5.
Mostly furniture.

Edward Joseph Antiques & Collectibles
520-522 Main St.
Phone (847) 332-1855
Mon. 4:30 to 6:30, Tues. thru Fri. 12:30 to 7:30,
Sat. 12 to 6:30, Sun. 3:30 to 5:30.
Specializing old games, playing cards,
poker chips, mahjong, etc.

Village Bazaar Antiques
503 Main St. (east of Chicago Ave.)
Phone (847) 866-9444
Tuesday. thru Friday 12 to 6, Sat. 12 to 4.
Bob Zidek has everything from furniture to
jewelry, including toys, china, crystal.

British Collectibles of Chicago
917 Chicago Ave.
Phone (847) 570-4867
Monday thru Saturday 9:30 to 6, Sun. 12:30 to 4.
New and old Toby jugs, estate jewelry, antique
furniture. David Winter cottages. 3 rooms are the
home of the American Toby Jug Museum, meticu-
lously arranged and labeled.

Fabola
1041 Chicago Ave.
Phone (847) 864-3880
Mon. thru Fri. 12 to 6, Thurs. 'til 8, Sat. 11 to 6,
Sunday 12 to 5.
Vintage clothing, jewelry, furniture, resale.

Harvey Antiques
1231 Chicago Ave.
Phone (847) 866-6766
Tuesday thru Saturday 11 to 5.
18th & 19th C. American furnishings, folk art,
superb antique jewelry. American Indian items.

Another Time, Another Place Antiques
1243 Chicago Ave.
Phone (847) 866-7170
Monday thru Saturday 10 to 4.
Furniture, jewelry, linens, quilts.

EVANSTON *(continued)*

Secret Treasures
1304 Chicago Ave.
Phone (847) 866-6889
Tues. thru Fri. 11 to 6, Sat. 10 to 5, Sun. 12 to 5.
*Consignment shop of antiques, collectibles, gifts
and accessories, from vintage to contemporary.*

FolkWorks Gallery
1310-1/2 Chicago Ave.
Phone (847) 328-0083
Tuesday thru Saturday 11 to 5, Sun. 1 to 5.
*Folk art, one of a kind, decorative arts, country
antiques. Bakelite jewelry. A unique new show
opens every month.*

Sarah Bustle Antiques, Ltd.
821 Dempster St.
Phone (847) 869-7290
Monday thru Saturday 10 to 6, closed Wed.
Sunday 1 to 4,
*Wonderful antique lighting, jewelry, and more.
Readers of* North Shore *Magazine voted it the best
antique shop on the north shore. Congratulations!*

EVANSTON *(continued)*

The Pursuit of Happiness
1524 Chicago Ave.
Phone (847) 869-2040
Monday thru Saturday 11 to 6.
Antiques, decorative arts, paintings, ethnic art.

Hiltie's
1812 Central St. (east of the viaduct)
Phone (847) 492-1001
Tuesday thru Saturday 11 to 5.
Mission furniture completely restored.

Morton Grove

Magazine Memories
6006 Dempster St. (at Austin)
Phone (847) 470-9444
Mon. thru Fri. 11 to 7, Sat. 10 to 6, Sun. 12 to 5.
100,000 magazines that go back to 1840. Original newspapers from 1740. 10,000 posters.

Wilmette

Al-Bar-Wilmette Platers
127 Green Bay Rd.
Phone (847) 251-0187
Monday thru Friday 8 to 5, Sat. 8 to 3.
Although their main business is metal finishing, they sell antique lighting and silver and brass decorative accessories, door hardware, etc.

Shorebirds
415-1/2 Fourth St.
Phone (847) 853-1460
Tuesday thru Saturday 10 to 5:30.
Painted furniture, linens, vintage textiles.

Buggy Wheel Antiques
1143 Greenleaf Ave.
Phone (847) 251-2100
Tuesday thru Saturday 10 to 4.
Buggy Wheel has been in business for 36 years.

Elizabeth Ferguson, Inc.
1135 Greenleaf Ave.
Phone (847) 853-0580
Tuesday thru Saturday 11 to 4.
Antique prints, original book illustrations—many relating to children.

The Crystal Cave
1141 Central Ave.
Phone (847) 251-1160
Monday thru Friday 10 to 6, Saturday 9 to 5.
Glass repair and engraving. Fine selection of new glass and porcelain.

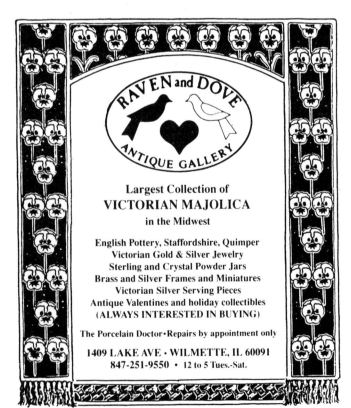

WILMETTE *(continued)*

Antiques & Jewelry by Weber
1129 Central St.
Phone (847) 251-1572
Tuesday thru Saturday 10 to 6.
Antiques, fine jewelry including estate diamonds.

West End Antiques
619 Green Bay Rd. (South of Lake Ave.)
Phone (847) 256-2291
Tuesday thru Saturday 10:30 to 5.
Oriental, Tribal and Pre-Columbian.
A new location for this shop.

The Collected Works
1405 Lake Ave. (near corner of Green Bay Rd.)
Antique shop: (847) 251-6897
Tuesday thru Saturday 12 to 5.
Repair shop: (847) 251-6898
Tuesday thru Saturday 9:30 to 5.
The shop is filled with their specialty: fine old wicker
and they also have antique beds, decorative
accessories, garden furniture, etc. Wicker repair.

21
VIDEOS
ABOUT ANTIQUES
"Doorways To The Past"

A unique series developed by
the educational film committee
of the Wisconsin Antique
Dealers Association.

Videos 30/40 minutes-$16.50:
Queen Anne Chairs
Early American Pressed Glass I
Early American Pressed Glass II
Fakes & Reproductions
Made in Milwaukee
Lalique Glass
Norwegian Antiques in Wisconsin
Introduction to Prints
Tobacco Antiques/Collectibles
Garden Furniture & Artifacts
Wrought Iron by Cyril Colnik
Wisconsin Heritage-Part I
Wisconsin Heritage-Part II
Wisconsin Heritage-Part III

Videos 50/60 minutes-$26.45:
Wisconsin Heritage-Part IV
American Indian Artifacts
150 Years of Haviland China
Introduction to Early China
Popular Victorian China
16th C-20th C Scent Bottles
Antique Toys

To order a brochure describing
the videos in detail, send a Self-
Addressed Stamped Envelope to the
address below.

To order Videos: Add $1.50 postage and handling for each
video. Make check payable to WADA Educational Film
Committee. Send order to SHARRON CYPHER,
135 N. MAIN ST., HARTFORD, WI 53027.
Phone (414) 673-2751

72

WILMETTE *(continued)*

Raven & Dove Antique Gallery
1409 Lake Ave. (near corner of Green Bay Rd.)
Phone (847) 251-9550
Tuesday thru Saturday 12 to 5.
A charming shop featuring majolica, jewelry,
miniatures, Staffordshire, Quimper, etc.
Not to be missed.

Heritage Trail Mall
410 Ridge Rd. (Green awning on north east corner
 of Ridge & Wilmette Ave.)
Phone (847) 256-6208
Monday thru Saturday 10 to 5:30, Sun. 12 to 5.
The building once housed the Hoffman Bros. Dry
Goods & Feed Store. The mall has expanded
into the adjacent 2 story brick stable.

Josie's
545 Ridge Rd.
Phone (847) 256-7646
Tues. Wed. 11 to 5, Thurs. Fri. Sat. 12 to 6,
Sunday 12 to 4.
20th C, art deco & nouveau. Small furniture, jewelry.

Smith and Ciffone Antiques

An eclectic collection of period
and decorative furniture,
Staffordshire, Majolica, English
and Continental pottery and porcelain,
antique accessories and
Victorian oddities.

630 Green Bay Rd • Kenilworth, IL 60043
847•853•0234

Monday thru Saturday
11 a.m. to 5 p.m.

WE BUY
Estates or
Single Items

Kenilworth

The Federalist Antiques
515 Park Drive
Phone (847) 256-1791
Monday thru Saturday 10 to 5.
American period furniture, period accessories and works of art.

Georgette Antiques
523 Park Drive
Phone (847) 251-7101
Tuesday thru Saturday 10:30 to 4:30.
English and American 18th & 19th C. furniture, carpets and paintings.

Smith & Ciffone Antiques
630 Green Bay Rd. (white building, 2 blocks south of Winnetka Ave.)
Phone (847) 853-0234
Monday thru Saturday 11 to 5.
Tony and Michelle have moved next door into a larger building. You'll always find interesting antiques here.

76

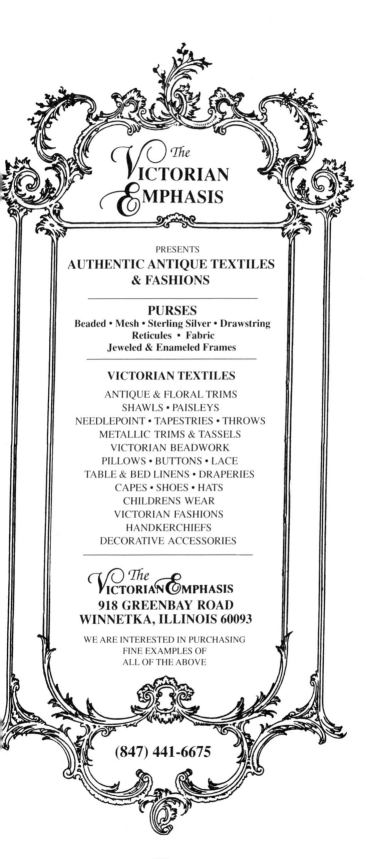

77

78

KENILWORTH *(continued)*

Kenilworth Antiques Center
640 Green Bay Rd. Watch for the
butter yellow awning.
Phone (847) 251-8003
Monday thru Saturday 11 to 5.
Furniture and smalls in this charming shop.

Edward Bania Fine Art
640 Green Bay Rd.
Phone (847) 446-6644
Monday thru Saturday 11 to 5.
Antique prints, picture framing and smalls.

Winnetka

Country Shop
710-12 Oak St.
Phone (847) 441-8690
Tuesday thru Saturday 10 to 5.
Country decor - a handsome shop.

M. Stefanich Antiques, Ltd.
549 Lincoln Ave.
Phone (847) 446-4955
Tuesday thru Saturday 10 to 5.
*Antique English silver, Old Sheffield plate,
Victorian plate, antique brass and copper,
Chinese export porcelain.*

Pied-À-Terre
554 Lincoln Ave.
Phone (847) 441-5161
Tuesday thru Saturday 10:30 to 4:30.
French country furniture.

Caledonian, Inc.
562 Lincoln Ave.
Phone (847) 446-6566
Tuesday thru Saturday 9 to 5.
18th & 19th C. English furniture & accessories.

WINNETKA *(continued)*

Heather Higgins Antiques
567 Lincoln Ave.
Phone (847) 446-3455
Monday thru Saturday 10:30 to 5.
English & American furniture. English blue & white china, Staffordshire figures, paintings.

Robertson-Jones Antiques
569 Lincoln Ave.
Phone (847) 446-0603
Monday thru Saturday 10:30 to 5:30.
18th & 19th C. English formal & country furniture. Boxes, mirrors, display cases.

Donald Stuart Antiques
571 Lincoln Ave.
Phone (847) 501-4454
Monday thru Saturday 10 to 5.
Antique silver, period furniture, Staffordshire, porcelain. A fine antique shop.

And in Hubbard Woods *(north Winnetka, just north of Tower Rd.)*

Arts 220
895$\frac{1}{2}$ Green Bay Rd.
Phone (847) 501-3084
Tuesday thru Saturday 11 to 4, or by appointment.
An interesting 2 blocks of antiques shops starting with Arts 220. Fern Simon specializes in Arts & Crafts, Art Deco and postwar jewelry, metalwork and pottery. Major examples of mid-century furniture.

Greenhouse
897$\frac{1}{2}$ Green Bay Rd.
Phone (847) 441-8808
Tuesday thru Saturday 10 to 5.
Indoor and outdoor antiques with a garden motif.

WINNETKA *(continued)*

Knightsbridge Antiques
909 Green Bay Rd.
Phone (847) 441-5105
Tuesday thru Saturday 11 to 4:30.
18th & early19th C. English furniture and fine
accessories. Chinese export porcelain, British pottery
& porcelain.

Hubbard Woods Antiques
913 Green Bay Rd.
Phone (847) 446-4353
Tuesday thru Saturday 11 to 5.
Arts & crafts and mission style furniture
and accessories.

The Antique Emporium
915 Green Bay Rd.
Phone (847) 446-0584
Monday thru Friday 9:30 to 5:30, Sat. 10 to 5.
English and French country furniture.

The Victorian Emphasis
918 Green Bay Rd.
Phone (847) 441-6675
Tuesday, Wednesday, Friday, Saturday 11:30 to 5.
An extensive selection of wonderful antique textiles,
purses and accessories. A treasure trove of textures—
the selection is overwhelming.

Ken Young Antiques & Collectibles
920 Green Bay Rd.
Phone (847) 441-6670
Tuesday thru Saturday 10 to 5.
Fine antique jewelry, antique watches, sterling
silver flatware & hollowware.

The Bellows Shoppe, Inc.
1060 Gage St.
Phone (847) 446-5533
Monday thru Friday 9 to 5, Sat. 9 to 4.
They are a metal restoration shop but, they also sell
chandeliers, wall sconces, lighting fixtures,
Victorian, mission, art nouveau, art deco.
Door & window hardware, floor & table lamps.

Bick's
964$^{1}/_{2}$ Green Bay Rd.
Phone (847) 441-7744
Monday thru Saturday 10 to 5.
Coins, baseball cards, jewelry-and
lots of collectibles.

WINNETKA *(continued)*

Antique Heaven & Ile de France
982 Green Bay Rd.
Phone (847) 446-0343
Monday thru Friday 11 to 5, Sat. 10 to 5.
Consignments of antique furniture, china, glass,
silver. Ile de France imports antique furniture
and accessories.

Northfield

Crost Furniture & Imports
1799 Willow Rd.(1 block west of the
Edens Expressway.)
Phone (847) 501-2550
Monday thru Friday 9:30 to 5, Sat. 9 to 5:30.
Imports from England, interesting accessories and
antique reproductions.

Town & Country Antiques
310 Happ Rd. (1 block south of Willow Rd.)
Phone (847) 501-4902
Monday thru Friday 11 to 5, Sat. 11 to 4.
Located in a charming shop that overlooks a
brick courtyard and fountain. Beautiful
selection of antiques will be found here.

Glenview

Antiques and Porcelain by G. K. Ltd.
1011 Harlem Ave. (at Glenview Rd.)
Phone (847) 724-3059
Tuesday thru Saturday 10:30 to 5.
Meissen, continental and English antique pottery
and porcelain, European glass, bronzes. Their
selection of Meissen is breathtaking.

Glencoe

International Silverplating & Antiques
364 Park Ave.
Phone (847) 835-0705
Tues. thru Fri. 9 to 4:30, Sat. 9 to noon.
A metal restoration shop with a locksmith who will
repair troublesome antique hardware, locks
without keys, etc. They also have a fine selection of
brass, copper, silver antiques including antique
Judaica.

It's About Time
375 Park Ave.
Phone (847) 835-2012
Wednesday thru Saturday 10 to 5.
Antique clocks.

Highland Park

Titles, Inc.
1931 Sheridan Rd.
Phone (847) 432-3690
Monday thru Saturday 10:30 to 5.
Antiquarian and rare books.

Arthur M. Feldman Gallery
1815 St. Johns Ave.
Phone (847) 432-8858
Monday thru Saturday 10 to 5.
Antiques, fine art, jewelry, Judaica.

Highwood

Jerry Lee Antiques
316 Green Bay Rd.
Phone (847) 432-2177
Monday thru Friday 7 pm to 9 pm,
Saturday 2 to 9, & Sunday 2 to 5:30.
*Antique wrist and pocket watches, antique
jewelry, clocks, toys, etc.*

Freidarica, Ltd. Antiques
257 Waukegan Ave. (in downtown Highwood.)
Phone (847) 433-4595 or 432-7749
*English & French accessories: earthenware,
brass, copper, boxes, decorative accessories.*

Lake Forest

Olden Daze Antique Jewelers
514 N. Western Ave.
Phone (847) 295-3333
Thurs., Fri., Sat. 10 to 4, Sun. 10 to 2.
*Marvelous selection of fine jewelry - usually
you'll find not one, but a dozen
examples of what you are looking for.*

The Clockworks
560 N. Western Ave.
Phone (847) 234-7272
Monday thru Friday 9 to 5:30, Sat. 9 to 4.
Antique clocks.

Crescent Worth Art & Antiques
626 N. Western Ave.
Phone (847) 295-8036, Fax: 295-8145
Mon. thru Sat. 10 to 5:30, open some Sundays.
*A wide range of antiques for the collector
and decorator. Choose from over 100 period
paintings.*

LAKE FOREST *(continued)*

Spruce Antiques
740 N. Western Ave.
Phone (847) 234-1244
Monday thru Saturday 10 to 4.
*18th & early 19th C. English and continental
furniture and accessories.*

The Country House
179 E. Deerpath Rd.
Phone (847) 234-0244
Monday thru Friday10 to 5, Sat. 10 to 4.
"Antique furnishings and fitments since 1936."

The Country Cottage
586 Bank Lane (lower level. Use American
Express Travel entrance.)
Saturdays 10 to 4.
*English oak, Staffordshire. Wicker, Jewelry, pocket
watches, clocks.*

Samlesbury Hall, Ltd.
730 Forest Ave.
Phone (847) 295-6070
Monday thru Saturday 9 to 5.
*17th & 18th C. English furniture,
antique porcelain, crystal, silver, prints.
Celebrating their 15th anniversary.*

Snow-Gate Antiques
234 E. Wisconsin
Phone (847) 234-3450
Tues. thru Sat.10 to 4:45, call for Mon. & Wed. hours.
*You can't resist browsing through the
two rooms of jewelry, glassware, etc.*

89

LAKE FOREST *(continued)*

Anna's Mostly Mahogany
950 N. Western Ave.
Phone (847) 295-9151
Monday thru Saturday 10 to 5, Sun. 11 to 4.
Elegant and attractive antique and vintage estate furniture, polished to perfection. Beautiful accessories.

Lake Forest Antique Consignment, Inc.
950 N. Western Ave.
Phone (847) 234-0442
Tuesday thru Saturday 10 to 5.
The shop is filled with splendid furniture, paintings, crystal and silver from local estates.

David O'Neill Antiques
Phone (847) 234-9344 - by appointment only.
18th C. furniture, folk art, porcelains, etc. Many unusual pieces, you could call them unique—I know the word (unique) is overused, but it fits.

Lake Bluff

The Shops on Scranton
37 E. Scranton Ave.
Phone (847) 735-0001
Monday thru Friday 10 to 5, Sat. 'til 4.
The Tribune called it "an eclectic haven for jewelry, antiques, ironwork, watercolors, hand-carved and painted furniture and one-of-a-kind art."

Lawrence Interiors, Inc.
109 E. Scranton Ave.
Phone (847) 234-7944
Monday thru Friday 9 to 5, Sat. 'til 4.
English furniture, reproductions and accessories, autograph gallery.

Waukegan

The Antique Connection
608 & 612 North Ave.
Phone (847) 623-4008
Tuesday thru Saturday 1 to 6.
Fanciful wares from a more elegant time.

Ancestor's
709 North Ave.
Phone (847) 623-4700
Monday thru Saturday 12 to 5.
A little bit of everything.

Armstrong's Second Connection
2823 Sunset (N. of Grand, off Green Bay Rd.)
Phone (847) 263-8246
Monday thru Saturday 10 to 6.
Furniture, collectibles, depression glass, jewelry.

West of Gurnee

Anamosa Antiques

On Rt. 132, 1 block west of Rt. 45 (19056 W. Grand)
Phone (847) 356-0832
Tuesday thru Sunday 10 to 5.
*Specializing in furniture, the shop also has
glassware, toys, militaria. Laura Murphy named
her shop after the Iowa hometown of her grandfather.*

Grayslake

Antique Warehouse of Grayslake

2 S. Lake St., just off Rt. 120.
Phone (847) 223-9554
Monday thru Saturday 10 to 5, Sun. 12 to 5.
Open 10 to 5 the 2nd Sunday of every month.
*You won't want to miss this 65-dealer mall in the
historic Cupola Building in the heart of Grayslake.*

Duffy's Attic

22 Center St.
Phone (847) 223-7454
Tuesday thru Saturday 10 to 5, Sun. 12 to 4.
*2 floors full of glassware, clocks, furniture,
in a 100-year old Victorian house.*

Yesterday Once More

299 Belvidere Rd. (Rt. 120) 1 mile west of Rt. 83.
Phone (847) 543-1415. Open 7 days 10 to 5.
Depression glass, furniture, coins, stamps, toys.

SHOW: Antique Show & Sale. "Grayslake Show"
at the Lake County Fairground, Rt. 45 & Rt. 120,
2nd Sunday of each month 8 am to 4 pm.

Hainesville

The Country Boutique

On Rt. 120 and Hainesville Rd.
Phone (847) 223-2452 or (847) 546-4295
Most Saturdays & Sundays 12 to 4, or by appt.
Delightful country shop.

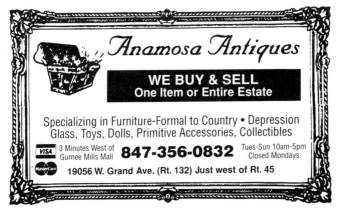

Fox Lake

Antique Alley Mall
415 S. Washington St.
Phone (847) 587-0091
Mon. Tues. Fri. 11 to 5, Sat. & Sun. 10 to 4,
closed Wed. Thurs.
*Appropriately named (located in a former bowling
alley) the mall is located a famous boating area.*

Lil Bit O'Everything, Inc.
48 E. Grand Ave.
Phone (847) 973-2912
Mon. thru Fri. 10 to 5, closed Wed. Sat. Sun. 11 to 4.
Resale & antiques, furniture, household items.

Antioch

Park Avenue Antique Mall
345 Park Ave. (3rd street north of the Rts. 173 & 83
intersection)
Phone (847) 838-1624
7 days, 10 to 5.
*Ramble thru this interesting mall, don't miss any of
the rooms and nooks and crannies and specialty
collections.*

Williams Bros. Emporium
910 Main St. (Rt. 83)
Phone (847) 838-2767
Monday thru Saturday 10 to 5, Sun. 12 to 5.
*Located in the 1892 building on Main St., the
Emporium offers furniture, stained glass windows,
built-ins, pier mirrors.*

Green Bench Antiques
924 Main St. (Rt. 83)
Phone (847) 838-2643
Tuesday thru Saturday 10 to 4, Fri. 'til 7.
Antiques, collectibles, smalls, decorative items.

The Collection Connection
400 W. Lake, 1 block north of Main St. (Rt. 83).
Phone (847) 395-8800
Tuesday thru Sunday 10 to 5, Friday 'til 6,
Filled to overflowing with cherished knicknacks.

The Dairy Barn
23 North Ave. (east of Rt. 83)
Phone (847) 838-6011
Wed. thru Fri. 9 to 5, Sat. & Sun. 8 to 4.
Antiques and crafts.

Another Man's Treasure
25218 Rt. 173 (2 miles west of Rt. 83)
Phone (847) 395-8513
Wednesday thru Sunday 10 to 5.
*Country kitchen items, oil & electric lamps,
primitives, stoneware, furniture.*

Antioch *(continued)*

Channel Lake School Antique & Collectible Mall
Lake Ave. & Rt. 173 (3-1/2 miles west of Rt. 83)
Phone (847) 395-0000 (that's it-believe me)
Wednesday thru Sunday 10 to 5.
It's not hard to imagine this 1930 school filled with children instead of antiques and collectibles.

Millburn

Martin's Gen'l Store
38757 N. Hwy. 45
Saturday and Sunday 12:30 to 4. Closed Jan. & Feb.
A general store since 1862, one of 18 structures in Millburn on the National Register of Historic Landmarks.

Zion

Zion Antique Mall
2754 Sheridan Rd.
Phone (847) 731-2060
Tues. thru Sat. 9:30 to 5, Sun. 1 to 5.
6 dealers.

For Wisconsin shops north of Illinois border, see page 168.

Area 3
NEAR NORTH PROVINCES

In this section: Wheeling, Prairie View, Lincolnshire, Half-Day, Libertyville, Mundelein, Long Grove, Lake Zurich, Wauconda, Hawthorne Woods, Volo.

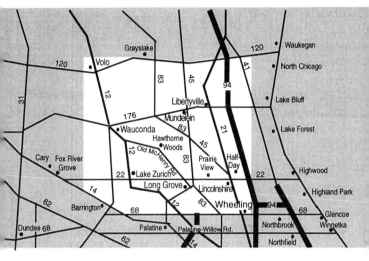

Wheeling

Antiques Center of Illinois
1920 S. Wolf Rd. (NW corner of Wolf & Camp McDonald Rd.)
Phone (847) 215-9418
7 days, 10 to 5.
A light and spacious mall filled with the antiques and collectibles of 58 dealers.

Sale Barn Square
971 N. Milwaukee Ave. (N. of Lake-Cook Rd.)
Originally the homestead of the Redlinger family. It's hard to believe this quiet complex of buildings, nestled under the trees, is just off a busy highway.

Wheeling Sale Barn
Phone (847) 537-9886
7 days, 9 to 5.
Furniture, china, chairs in the loft.

Lundgren's
Antiques & Distinctive Accessories
Phone (847) 541-2299
Tues. thru Sun. 11 to 5, in winter: 10:30 to 4.

Antiques of Northbrook
in the 1835 Aptakisic Tripp Schoolhouse.
Phone (847) 215-4994
7 days, 10 to 5.
Antiques & collectibles, jewelry, furniture.

Wheeling *(continued)*

Sale Barn Square *(continued)*

My Favorite Place Antiques & Echoes Antiques
Phone (847) 808-1324
7 days, 10 to 5.
Antique linens, vintage jewelry, chandeliers & lamps, sets of tableware, vintage clothing.

County Faire, Inc.
Phone (847) 537-9987
7 days, 10 to 5.
The big red farmhouse is filled with antiques and collectibles, furniture, books, etc. All the rooms are filled.

O'Kelly's Art, Antiques & Jewelry
Phone (847) 537-1656
Tuesday thru Sunday 11 to 5.
Art, antiques, jewelry, fine glassware. Small, carved, wooden carousel horses.

Shirley's Doll House
Phone (847) 537-1632
Monday thru Saturday 10 to 5, Sun. 11 to 4.
Old and new dolls, accessories. Teddy bears.

The Crystal Magnolia
Phone (847) 537-4750
Tuesday thru Sunday 10 to 5.
Permanent floral arrangements, cookie jars, antiques and collectibles.

Kerry's Clock Shop
in the 1835 farmhouse.
Phone (847) 520-0335
Tues. thru Sat. 10 to 5, Sun. by chance or appt.
Antique wall, shelf, cuckoo, regulator, etc. clocks for sale. Antique clock repair.

Prairie View

White Elephant Shop
23042 N. Main St. (1 mile west of Half-Day on Rt. 22, then 1 block north, west side of tracks.)
Phone (847) 634-3415
Tuesday thru Sunday 10 to 5.
Furniture, jewelry, much miscellaneous. It's a short jaunt west of Milwaukee Ave.

The Calendar of Antique Shows begins on page 247.

Lincolnshire

Rebecca Anne Antiques / Lincolnshire
On the west side of Milwaukee Ave. (Rt. 21),
just north of Rt. 22.
Phone (847) 634-2423
Mon. thru Fri. 10 to 6, Sat. 10 to 5, Sun. 12 to 5.
*Large shop filled with American and European
furniture. Pine. Buffets, armoires, carved
cabinets, desks and accessories.*

Half-Day

Phyllis Sibley Antiques
Milwaukee Ave. (Rt. 21) 1 mile north of Rt. 22.
Phone (847) 634-9177
Open most days 11 to 5.
*The shop has a variety of glass, china, etc. The
barn is filled with furniture and lighting fixtures.*

Libertyville

Neville-Sargent Gallery
406-410 N. Milwaukee Ave.
Phone (847) 680-1414
Mon. thru Fri. 11 to 6, Sat. 10 to 5, Sun. 12 to 3.
Furniture, sterling, accessories and an art gallery.

Armstrong's Country Connection
1757 N. Milwaukee Ave.
Phone (847) 816-8400
Monday thru Saturday 10 to 6, Sun. 11 to 5.
*Furniture, depression glass, books,
linens, dolls, lots of collectibles.*

Mundelein

Village Antique Mall
131 E. Maple (Rt. 176) 1 block east of Rt. 45.
Phone (847) 566-2363
Monday thru Saturday 10 to 5, Sun. 12 to 5.
Nice place to browse. 26 dealers fill the shop.

Long Grove

Bank Street Antiques
345 Old McHenry Rd., Fountain Square.
Phone (847) 634-0715
Monday thru Saturday 9:30 to 5, Sun. 12 to 5,
in winter: weekday hours 'til 4:30.
*Antique English country pine, Flow Blue,
china, Torquay, English pub signs.*

The Curiosity Shop of Long Grove
350 Old McHenry Rd.
Phone (847) 821-1877
Tuesday thru Saturday 10 to 5, Sun. 12 to 5.
Antique furniture in oak, walnut, mahogany.
Armoires. English & German porcelain, jewelry.

Klehm's Pink Peony Doll & Miniature
Shop & Doll Museum
250 Coffin Rd., Fountain Square, upstairs.
Phone (847) 634-6646
Monday thru Saturday 10 to 5, Sun. 11 to 5,
in winter: weekday hours 'til 4:30.
*Browse in the shop and treat yourself to a tour
of the museum. See dolls dating from 1834
thru the 1900's (and more).*

Long Grove *(continued)*

Especially Maine Antiques, Ltd.
Mill Pond Building - lower level.
Phone (847) 634-3512
Monday thru Saturday 10 to 5, Sun. 11 to 5.
Winter: weekdays 10:30 to 4:30, Sun. 11 to 5.
Penny's shop is filled with a wonderful mix of treasures for the serious and the "fun" collector.

The Emporium of Long Grove
Mill Pond - lower level
Phone (847) 634-0188
Monday thru Saturday 10 to 5, Sun. 12 to 5.
Winter: weekdays 10:30 to 4:30, Sun. 12 to 5.
This multi-dealer shop has an interesting mix of dealers.

The Hotel Shop (across from the Village Tavern)
146 Old McHenry Rd.
Phone (847) 821-9871
Tuesday thru Saturday 11 to 5, Sun. 12 to 5.
In winter: Wednesday thru Sunday 12 to 5.
Country and Victorian furniture, English and American china, jewelry, primitives, vintage children's clothing, games and toys.

Carriage Trade
427 Coffin Rd. - 3rd from the bridge.
Phone (847) 634-3160
Tuesday thru Saturday 11 to 5.
*Pine: armoires, dressers, tables, chairs.
Oil paintings, rugs.*

Lake Zurich

The Antiques Shop
247 N. Rand Rd. (1 mile N. of Rt. 22, just south of stoplight at Ravinia Terr/Old Rand.
Phone (847) 438-0066
Monday thru Saturday 10 to 5.
General line.

Wauconda

Whippletree Farm Antiques
210 S. Main St.
Phone (847) 526-7808
Monday thru Saturday 10 to 5, Sun. by chance.
Two floors filled with a variety of antiques, including a large selection of furniture. In an old building (1906) formerly a hardware store.

Kramer's Country Casuals Antiques
109 S. Main St.
Phone (847) 526-7880
7 days, 10 to 5, closed Sundays in summer.
Estate jewelry, furniture, decorative accessories.

AUTO MUSEUM

3 ANTIQUE MALLS • 300 DEALERS
All connected plus
200 CAR FABULOUS AUTO MUSEUM
ALL FOR SALE
Internationally Famous
1 HOUR NORTH OF CHICAGO

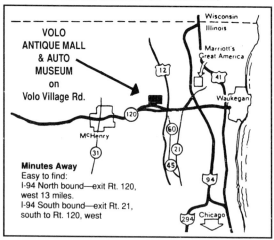

Now leasing - expanding Mall III. New Showcases
& Booths • You ship-we restock your case.

OLD VOLO VILLAGE
ANTIQUE 30 ACRE VILLAGE

OPEN 7 DAYS 10am to 5 pm
815-344-6062 • VOLO, ILLINOIS
Ask for Carolyn Grams, Mgr.

Hawthorne Woods

Colonial Antiques in the farmhouse. (1st driveway north of Old McHenry Rd.) 24675 Midlothian Rd.
Phone (847) 438-1932
Tuesday thru Sunday 10 to 5.
This is Lee Muto's shop filled with furniture, light fixtures, large restored cabinets and antiques, displayed in her own special way.

Volo

In the Old Volo Village on Rt. 120, 1/2 mile west of Rt. 12. Visit the car museum as well as the other shops.

Volo Antique Malls - 3 of them
Phone (815) 344-6062
7 days, 10 to 5.
Ramble thru the 100-year-old barn and connected buildings that are filled from top to bottom with the wares of 300 dealers.

Portobello Road Antiques
Phone (815) 385-6707
7 days, 11 to 5.
Primitives, jewelry, iron beds, furniture.

108

Area 4
NORTHWEST SUBURBS & YONDER

In this section: Chicago (Far northwest side), Park Ridge, Mt. Prospect, Schaumburg, Arlington Heights, Palatine, Barrington, Fox River Grove, Cary, Dundee (East & West), Elgin, Hampshire, Algonquin, Huntley, Union, Marengo, Crystal Lake, Ridgefield, Woodstock, McHenry, Richmond, Hebron, Harvard.

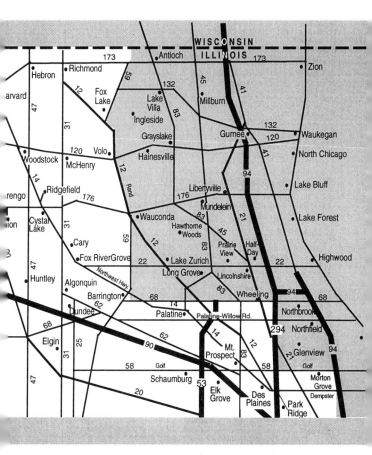

Chicago & Niles (Far northwest)

Gigi's Dolls & Sherry's Teddy Bears
6029 N. Northwest Hwy.
Phone (773) 594-1540 or 1-800-442-3655
Mon. thru Sat. 10 to 5, Thurs. & Fri. 'til 9,
Sunday 12 to 5.
If you haven't seen the shop, give yourself a treat.
A wonderland of dolls, dolls, dolls, teddy bears,
miniatures, etc.

110

CHICAGO / Niles *(continued)*

Calico Cat Antique & Resale
6046-48 N. Avondale (Avondale is 1 block
south of NW Hwy, parallel to the RR tracks.)
Phone (773) 774-3458
Mon. thru Fri. 11 to 3, Sat. by chance.
*Little of everything in the antique shop with a
tearoom featuring homemade food.*

Antique Picture Frames, Ltd.
7316 Milwaukee Ave.
Phone (847) 647-8467
Tuesday thru Friday 9 to 4, Sat. 'til 12.

The Antique & Resale Shop
7214 N. Harlem
Phone (773) 631-1151
Monday thru Saturday 10:30 to 4:30.
*Jam packed with collectibles, antiques
and costume jewelry.*

First Arts & Antiques
7220 W. Touhy
Phone (773) 774-5080
7 days: Mon. Tues. Thurs. 10 to 7,
Wed. Fri. Sat. 10 to 4, Sun. 12 to 4.

I Remember Mama
6122-24 N. Northwest Hwy.
Phone (773) 631-1301
Monday thru Friday 11 to 5, Sat. 11 to 3.
*Now a mini-mall with furniture,
tained glass, small tables, glassware.*

Little Ladies
6217 N. Northwest Hwy.
Phone (773) 631-3602
Tuesday thru Sunday 11 to 3.
Linens, furniture, books, hats.

Park Ridge

Boom Gallery
146 N. Northwest Hwy.
Phone (847) 823-2666
Mon. thru Fri.11 to 6, Sat. 10:30 to 6, Sun. 12 to 4.
Sat 10:30 to 6, Sun. 12 to 4.
*Specializing in baby boomer collectibles: 50's, 60's &
70's movie, TV, rock & roll, pop memoriabilia.
Also Lionel trains, etc.*

June Moon Collectibles
245 N. Northwest Hwy.
Phone (847) 825-1411
Tuesday thru Saturday 12 to 6.
*Collectible toys, paintings, pottery
and Star Wars.*

Mt. Prospect

Chelsea Gallerie
129 W. Prospect
Phone (847) 870-8332
Tuesday thru Friday 10 to 5, Sat. 'til 4.
Antique prints: Audubons, botanicals, hunt scenes.

Elk Grove Village

Oakton Street Antique Centre
2430 E. Oakton St. (2 blocks west of Elmhurst Rd.)
Phone (847) 437-2514
Monday thru Saturday 10 to 6, Sun. 11 to 6.
Large, spacious mall that is home to 70 dealers.

Antiques Mart of Elk Grove Village
1170 W. Devon Ave. (west of Arlington
Heights Rd., west of Rt. 53)
Phone (847) 895-8900
Mon. thru Fri. 11 to 7, Sat. & Sun. 10 to 5.
*Take time to browse the wares of 134
dealers.*

Antique Furniture Mart
adjacent to the Antiques Mart
Phone (847) 895-8900
Mon. thru Fri. 11 to 7, Sat. & Sun. 10 to 5.
Just opened, a large shop of antique furniture.

Schaumburg

The Estate in Woodfield Mall
Rt. 58 (Golf Rd.) just west of Rt. 53.
Nordstrom/Lord & Taylor wing.
Phone (847) 517-7750
Mon. thru Fri. 10 to 9, Sat. 10 to 7, Sun. 11 to 6.
*Who would have thought it? An antique shop in
Woodfield! They specialize in antique and estate
jewelry, but have lots of other antiques: silver, objects
d'art, Christmas tree ornaments, etc.*

Arlington Heights

Cobblestone Antiques
17 E. Miner (approx.1 block north of Northwest
Hwy., 1-1/4 blocks west of Arlington Hts. Rd.)
Phone (847) 259-4818
Tuesday 10 to 5, Thurs. 10 to 7, Sat. 10 to 5, other
days by chance.
*Invitingly cluttered and informal, Barbara's
shop specializes in fine silver. You'll love
browsing here.*

P.J.'s Antique & Collectibles
7 E. Miner St.
Phone (847) 259-7130
Tues. Wed. 10 to 5, Thurs. Fri. 10 to 7, Sat. 10 to 5.
Bottles, advertising, glassware, some furniture.

Arlington Heights *(continued)*

Museum Country Store
of the Arlington Heights Historical Society
112 W. Fremont St. (just west of library)
Phone (847) 255-1450
Thursday, Friday, Saturday 10 to 4, Sun. 1 to 4.
*Charming and brick floored, its antique
consignments are neatly displayed.*

Collage Antiques
1005 S. Arlington Hts. Rd. (just south of Central)
Phone (847) 439-5253
Monday thru Saturday 10 to 5, Sun. 12 to 5.
Two floors of antiques in the shopping center.

Palatine

Palatine Antique Center
23-25 E. Northwest Hwy. (Palatine Center Mall)
Phone (847) 359-9771
Monday thru Saturday 10 to 5, Sun. 11 to 5.
*This mall is in a shopping center set back
from the highway.*

Palatine *(continued)*

A Matter of Time
25 N. Brockway (downtown Palatine)
Phone (847) 359-1810
Tues. thru Sat. 11 to 5, longer holiday hours.
January & May, by appointment only.
Sell and repair fine antique clocks, pocket watches,
wristwatches, music boxes. They also sell antique accent
furniture, lamps, smalls.

Barrington

Estate Jewelers
118 W. Main St. (next to the Catlow Theatre)
Phone (847) 382-8802
Thursday, Friday, Saturday 11 to 5.
Fine vintage and antique jewelry, as well as
interesting collectibles.

Romantiques
118 W. Main St. • Phone (847) 304-9421 • Open daily.
Fine American & European furniture
and accessories. New shop opening in May.

Fresh Flower Market
122 W. Main St. • Phone (847) 381-7800
Monday thru Saturday 9 to 5.
Owner Iris has antique smalls and garden items.

115

Barrington *(continued)*

Silk 'n Things
308 W. Main St. (just west of downtown at Dundee St. stoplight.)
Phone (847) 381-3830
Monday thru Friday 10 to 5:30, Sat. 10 to 5.
Decorative antiques, linens and furniture accentuate the floral wonderland that fills every room of the 100 year old home.

Barrington Consignment Gallery
420 W. Northwest Hwy, 1/2 mile west of Rt. 59.
Phone (847) 304-0510
Tues. thru Fri. 10 to 6, Sat. 10 to 4, Sun. 12 to 4.
A consignment shop with a twist - prices descend monthly.

The Pink Geranium
829 W. Northwest Hwy. (1/4 mile west of Hart Rd., on south side of Rt. 14.)
Phone (847) 842-0115
Antique & vintage furniture, tables, lamps, linens, mirrors, etc. An imaginative collection.

Fox River Grove

Memories
412 N. Lincoln Ave.
Phone (847) 639-8555
Wednesday thru Saturday 11 to 4.
Just off of Rt. 14, the shop has an interesting and diversified stock.

Cary

Cary Station Antiques
22 Spring St.
Phone (847) 639-7434
By appointment.
Antiquities, curiosities, rarities, one-of a kind, oddities. Intriguing.

Dundee

The Antique Emporium at the Milk Pail
Rt. 25, 1/4 mile north of I-90
Phone (847) 468-9667
7 days 10 to 5.
50 dealers selling their antiques on two levels at this well known restaurant complex.

East Dundee

Windsor Antiques
205 S. Van Buren (2 blocks south of Rt. 72,
across from Haeger Potteries)
Phone (847) 428-0291
Saturday and Sunday, 10 to 4, weekdays by chance.
The living and dining room of this comfortable home has fine glass, porcelains, interesting small furniture and jewelry.

River St. Antiques & Gallery House
314 N. River St.
Phone (847) 426-3149
Thurs. Fri. Sat. 10:30 to 4:30.
Country antiques, primitives, collectibles.

Treasured Memories
1 E. Main St.
Phone (847) 428-1833
Monday thru Saturday 11 to 5, Sun. 12 to 4.
Furniture, glassware, Anna Lee dolls.

West Dundee (across the bridge)

Antiques & Decorative Arts of Dundee
105 W. Main St.
Phone (847) 426-0409
Thursday, Friday, Saturday 11 to 5.
Wyona Burns, a well known dealer, is the owner of this large shop featuring historical china and glass, porcelain, Americana, furniture, folk art, silver, garden and outdoor statuary.

Adornments
125 W. Main St.
Phone (847) 428-8323
Tues. Wed. Fri. Sat. 10:30 to 4:30, Sun. 12:30 to 4:30, closed Monday & Thursday.
Estate & antique jewelry, vintage linens. New clothing and gifts.

Elgin

Dunnings
755 Church Rd.
Phone (847) 741-3483
Auctions held monthly -call for their calendar.
Established in 1896, they have celebrated 100 years in business.

Hampshire

Old Saint Pete's Antiques
Rt. 47 & Plank Rd.
Phone (847) 464-0299 • 7 days 10 to 5.
32 dealers in the 128 year old church.

Algonquin

Algonquin Antique Mart
113 S. Main St.
Phone (847) 658-1991
Tuesday thru Sunday 10 to 4.
40 dealers.

Main Street Estates, Antiques & Collectibles
115 S. Main St.
Phone (847) 854-4444
Open 7 days 10 to 6.
A wonderful collection of antiques, cut glass, old prints, steins, etc. in downtown Algonquin.

Algonquin *(continued)*

Algonquin House Antiques
321 S. Main St.
Phone (847) 854-2504
Mon. thru Fri. 10 to 4, Sat. 10 to 5, Sun. 12 to 5.
Tools & primitives, glass, linens, vintage clothing.

Linden Gallery of Fine Art & Family Affair Antiques
213 S. Harrison (1 block east of Rt. 31)
Phone (847) 658-3666
7 days 10 to 4.
A gallery of paintings and prints and quality American antiques.

Collectors' Cupboard
401 Washington
Phone (847) 854-3776
Tuesday thru Sunday 10 to 4.
Furniture, collectibles, glassware.

Grandma's Attic

800 W Grant Hwy (Rt 20)
Marengo, Illinois 60152
815 568-2744

Tues - Fri 9 - 6   Sat 9 - 5
Sun 10 - 3   Closed Mon

Antiques * Collectibles * Clothing

Huntley

Youngstead Antiques & Uniques
7214 Seeman Rd. (3 miles east of Union)
Phone 815/923-4495
Usually open Tues. thru Sat. but best to call ahead.
Seek out this country shop. Graniteware
is their specialty.

Union

Donley's Wild West Town
8512 S. Union Rd.
Phone 815/923-2214
Open 7 days 10 to 6, Memorial Day thru Labor Day.
Weekends only in April, May & October.
A day in the country the whole family will enjoy—
take the kids and the seniors. A complex of
buildings and museum that will interest and amuse.

Village Trading Post
6504 Main St.
Phone 815/923-4162
Saturday and Sunday 10 to 5.
A few antiques, lots of second hand stuff.

Marengo

Grandma's Attic
800 W. Grant Hwy. (Business Rt. 20, 1/2 mile
west of McDonalds)
Phone 815/568-2744
Tues. thru Fri. 9 to 6, Sat. 9 to 5, Sun. 10 to 3.
Antique jewelry, antiques & collectibles, vintage
clothing.

Crystal Lake

Penny Lane Antiques & Associates
6114 Lou Ave. (1 block south of Rt. 14, off Teckler)
Phone 815/459-8828
Wednesday thru Sunday 11 to 5.
*Multi-dealer shop in this rambling building
filled with antiques and collectibles.*

Carriage Antiques
5111 East Rt. 176 (1 stoplight west of Rt. 31)
Phone 815/356-9808
Open 7 days, 10 to 5.
Furniture, glassware, primitives, collectibles.

Ridgefield

The Country Church
8509 Ridgefield Rd.
Phone 815/477-4601
Wednesday thru Sunday 11 to 4.
*Pine, oak, walnut, mahogany, English
pine furniture, folk art, textiles, old books,
china, glassware.*

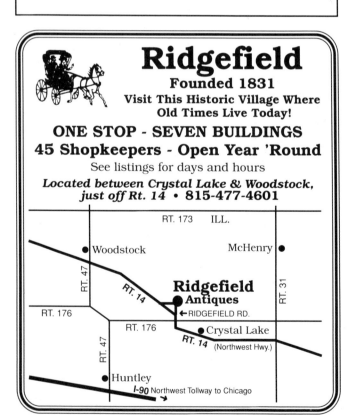

Ridgefield *(continued)*

Across the tracks:
Railroad Street Market
8316 Railroad St.
-look for the 3 old gas pumps in front of
the building on Railroad St.
Phone 815/459-4220
Wednesday thru Sunday 11 to 4.
7 dealers in the 1847 blacksmith and wagon-maker's shop featuring two floors of antique country pine, oak, walnut, mahogany furniture and accessories.

Aurora's Antiques
8404 Railroad St.
Phone 815/455-0710
Open 7 days, 11 to 5.
10 dealers in furniture, collectibles, glassware, jewelry, clocks, tools & farm primitives. American Girl doll dresses.

Postal Station
4124 Country Club Rd.
Phone 815/455-1834
Wednesday thru Sunday 11 to 4.
10 dealers & master artisans with antiques, furniture, florals, dolls, glass, ceramic & wood handcrafts. Furniture restoration and caning.

Antiques & Art Unlimited
4120 Country Club Rd.
Phone 815/356-9698
Wednesday thru Sunday 11 to 4.
An interesting mix of furniture, kitchenware, clocks and decorative pieces.

Way Back When Antiques
4112 Country Club Rd.
Phone 815/459-1360 or 815/338-9121
Wed. thru Fri. 11 to 4, Sat. & Sun. 11 to 5.
Specializing in custom barn board furniture, quilts, wicker, fiesta and chairs. Look for the white picket fence in front.

Woodstock

Interiors Anew
134 Cass St. "On the square"
Phone 815/337-9131
Monday thru Saturday 10 to 5, Sun. 11 to 4.
An interesting concept of recycled and redesigned furniture.

ANTIQUES

THE SHOPS
OF
RICHMOND
ILLINOIS

A RETURN TO YESTERYEAR

Centrally located and about an hour from Chicago, Milwaukee or Rockford, Richmond has over 20 quaint antique shops with some of the finest quality antiques you'll find anywhere. While you're here, visit one of the many fine restaurants and enjoy the historical buildings and homes in the area. Overnight lodging is also conveniently located.

Most of the shops are open daily 10:30 am to 5:00 pm year-round.

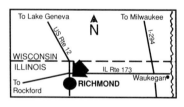

For more information, please call:
The Richmond Merchants Association
(815) 678-7951

Woodstock *(continued)*

Merchants Antique Mall
214 Main St. (just off the square-above the
Waverly House restaurant.)
Phone 815/337-0275
7 days 12 to 5.
18 dealers on 2 floors (2nd & 3rd) with furniture,
clocks, kitchenware, toys, games, dolls, etc.

McHenry

The Crossroad Merchant
1328 N. Riverside Drive (1 block N. of Rt. 120)
Phone 815/344-2610
Monday thru Saturday 10 to 4.
Delightfully different shop with quality antiques
nicely displayed.

Richmond

The Serendipity Shop
9818 Main St. (Rt. 12)
Phone 815/678-4141
Tuesday thru Sunday 10 to 5.
5 rooms of antiques.

Rustic American
10213 Main St.
Phone 815/678-2240
7 days 10:30 to 5.
Art, antiques, collectibles, memoribilia.

The 1905 Emporium
Southeast corner of Broadway & Main (Rt. 12)
Phone 815/678-4414
7 days, 10:30 to 5.
3 floors of glassware, jewelry, lighting,
advertising and country store items.

Antiques on Broadway
Southwest corner of Broadway St. & Main (Rt. 12)
Phone 815/678-7951
Tuesday thru Saturday 11 to 5, Sun. 12 to 5.
Winter weekdays 11 to 4.
Filled with fine refinished furniture including
dining room and bedroom sets. Also architectural
pieces. Lovely corner shop.

Little Bit Antiques
5603 Broadway St.
Phone 815/678-4218
7 days, 10:30 to 5.
The shop has a little bit of everything
including hanging light fixtures.

Richmond *(continued)*

The Olde Bank Antiques
5611 Broadway St.
Phone 815/678-4839
7 days, 11 to 5, Mon. & Tues. by chance in winter.
General line specializing in glassware,
paperweights, collector plates.

Hiram's Uptown
5613 Broadway St.
7 days, 10:30 to 5.
Phone 815/678-4166
Furniture, collectibles, old tools.

Cat's Stuff Antiques
In the white house near the bridge.
5627 Broadway
Phone 815/678-7807
Mon. thru Fri. 11 to 4, Sat. & Sun 11 to 5.
In the white house near the bridge.

A Step Above Antiques
5626 Broadway
Phone 815/678-6906
7 days 10 to 5.
Christmas room, some antiques, new southwest.

Kathleen's Lasting Treasures
5614 Broadway
Phone 815/678-4884
Wed. 12 to 5, Thurs. Fri. Sat. 10 to 5, Sun. 12 to 5,
closed Monday & Tuesday.
Antiques, home accessories and
select reproductions.

Discover
HEBRON
ILLINOIS

8 Antique Shops Within Walking Distance

Nancy Powers Antiques
12017 Maple St. (Rt. 173)
815/648-4804
Open Fri. thru Mon. 10-?
Quirky Country

Hebron Antique Gallery
10002 Main Street
815/648-4794
Open Daily 10-5
Architectural • Garden
Primitives

**Lloyd & Leota's
Antiques & Restoration**
10103 Main Street
815/648-2202
Open Daily 9-4:30
Antiques and Fine Furniture
Handstripping • Complete
Restoration Service

**Prairie Avenue
Antiques**
Corner Main & Prairie
815/648-4507
Open Daily 10-5
Collectables • Antique Furniture
& Accessories

Scarlet House
9911 Main Street
815/648-4112
Open Daily 10-5 • Closed Tue.
Eclectic Mix of Primitives
& Country

Grampy's Antique Store
10003 Main Street
815/648-2244
Open Daily 10-5
Closed Tue. & Wed.
Antique Furniture
Primitives

Back In Time
10004 Main Street
815/648-2132
Open Daily 11-4
Closed Mon. & Tue.
Uniques • Primitives • Victoriana

Watertower Antiques
9937 Main Street
815/648-2287
Hours Vary
Antiques & Collectables

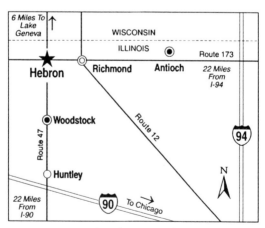

*Spend a day in Hebron !
Several nice restaurants nearby.*

Richmond *(continued)*

Karin Lynn's Antiques / Village Bookstore
5612 Broadway St.
Phone 815/678-2528
Open weekends, enter thru Purdy's.
American primitives.

The Happy House
5604 Broadway St.
Phone 815/678-4076
7 days, 10:30 to 5.
Pocket watches, jewelry, clocks.

Marilyn's Touch
10315 Main St. (northwest corner of Broadway)
Phone 815/678-7031
7 days, 10:30 to 5. In winter open Wednesday
thru Sunday.
Jewelry, furniture.

Ed's Antiques
10321 Main St. (Rt. 12)
Phone 815/678-2911
Tuesday thru Saturday 10:30 to 5, Sun. 12 to 5.
Three floors filled with antique furniture,
old stained & beveled glass, etc.

The Rose Peddler's Wife & Co.
10327 Main St. (Rt. 12)
Phone 815/678-3802
Tuesday thru Saturday 11 to 5, Sun. 12 to 5.
2 floors of antiques, linens, art pottery, furniture.

Hebron

Nancy Powers Antiques
12017 Maple St. (corner of Rt. 173 & 47)
Phone 815/648-4804
Open Friday thru Monday.
Quirky country stuff.

Back in Time Antiques
10004 Main St.
Phone 815/648-2132
Wednesday thru Sunday 11 to 4.
Victoriana, primitives, glassware.

Hebron Antique Gallery
10002 Main St.
Phone 815/648-4794
7 days, 10 to 5.
Quality furniture, folk art, fine art,
architectural and garden antiques,
primitives.

Hebron *(continued)*

Prairie Avenue Antiques
Corner of Prairie & Main St.
Phone 815/648-4507
Open 7 days 10 to 5.
Collectibles, antique furniture and accessories.

Scarlet House Antiques
9911 Main St.
Phone 815/648-4112
6 days 10 to 5, closed Tuesday.
A mix of primitives and country.

Water Tower Antiques
9937 Main St.
Phone 815/648-2287
Antiques & collectibles.

Grampy's Antique Store
10003 Main St.
Phone 815/648-2244
5 days 10 to 5, closed Tuesday & Wednesday.
*Housed in one of Hebron township's olderst buildings,
the turn-of -the-century department store is now the
home of many well known antiques dealers.
Don't miss it.*

Lloyd & Leota's Antiques & Restoration
10103 Main St.
Phone 815/648-2202
7 days 9 to 4:30.
*Antiques and fine furniture. Handstripping and
omplete restoration service.*

Harvard

Dairy Barn Antiques
708 W. Brink St. (Rt. 173) 1/4 mile west of Rt. 14.
Phone 815/943-7030
7 days, 10 to 5.
A multi-dealer mall in the converted dairy barn.
Dealers feature glass, Griswold, furniture, bottles,
steins, tools, books, marbles and more.

Beverly's Room
8106 Reese Rd.
Phone 815/943-5643
Sat. & Sun. 10 to 5, weather permitting, best to
call ahead.
Collectibles, some furniture, antiques.

For Wisconsin shops just north of Harvard and
the Illinois border see Walworth, Wisconsin, page 174.

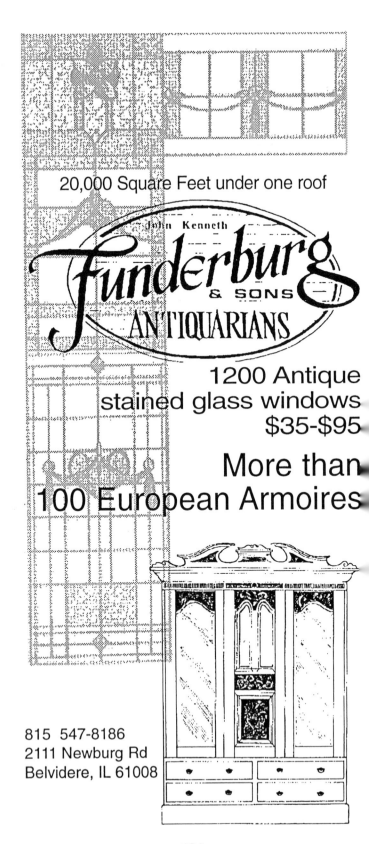

Area 5
NORTHERN ILLINOIS

In this section: Belvidere, Rockford, Machesney Park, Rockton, Pecatonica, Seward, Leaf River, Freeport, Eleroy, Lena, Pearl City, Stockton, Warren, Elizabeth, Galena. Stillman Valley, Oregon, Dixon, Sterling, Rock Falls, Morrison, Savanna and Maquoketa, Iowa.

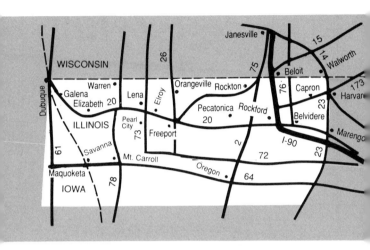

Belvidere

John Kenneth Funderburg & Sons
2111 Newburg Rd.
Phone 815/547-8186
Tuesday thru Saturday 10 to 5, Sun. 12 to 5.
Only slightly smaller than an airplane hanger but considerably nicer, filled with English and American furniture and lots of stained glass windows.

The Home Place Antiques
615 So. State St.
Phone 815/544-0577 or 815/547-5128
Tuesday thru Saturday 10 to 5, Sundays & evenings by appt. Jan. & Feb.: call advised.
Specializing in lamps, period lighting, Tea Leaf Ironstone. Also a general line of quality antiques.

Wooden-It-Be-Nice
419 E. Pleasant
Phone 815/544-0249
Mon. thru Sat. 9 to 6, but best to call first.
Specializing in furniture, old signs, advertising and Coca-Cola items.

EAST STATE STREET

Antique Malls

I & II

in ROCKFORD, ILLINOIS

...at 60,000 sq. ft.
we are the
midwest's largest!

Over
320 QUALITY DEALERS

Hundreds of pieces of fine furniture, country furnishings primitives, art deco, lots of colorful old advertising, slot machines, clocks, fine china, pottery. . . and much more!

**2-DAY OUTDOOR
ANTIQUE MARKETS**
in our parking lots
Rain or Shine! Open 8 am
**1997: May 25-26•July 5-6
Aug 31-Sept 1**
FREE ADMISSION
Dealers call for details

OPEN 7 DAYS 10 to 9

TWO GIANT LOCATIONS

MALL I	MALL II
5411 E. State St.	5301 E. State St.
(815)229-4004	(815) 226-1566

Rockford, Illinois 61108

1,000 parking stalls

Rockford

Barbara A. Johnson Antiques & Gifts
7801 E. State St. (I-90 & Bus. Rt. 20,
Clock Tower Inn) Phone 815/397-6699
7 days, 10 to 5.
Beautiful shop, antiques, Scandinavian antiques and lots of new folk art.

East State Street Antiques Mall I
5411 E. State St. (On Bus. Rt. 20) lower level
of New Towne Plaza I
Phone 815/229-4004
7 days, 10 to 9.
320 dealers in this original mall and their sister shop, Mall II.

East State Street Antiques Mall II
5301 E. State St. (Bus. Rt. 20) lower level of
New Towne Plaza II
Phone 815/226-1566
7 days, 10 to 9.
The antiques business is in full swing at these two giant shops.

Rockford *(continued)*

Vignettes
1680 N. Alpine Rd. (in High Crest Center, lower level)
Phone 815/399-6610
Tues. thru Fri. 11 to 5:30, Sat. 9:30 to 5, Sun. 11 to 2.
China, crystal, silver, jewelry, fine furniture.

Forgotten Treasures Antiques & Gifts
4610 E. State St. (across from Sweden House Lodge)
Phone 815/229-0005
Monday thru Friday 10 to 6, Sat. 10 to 5.
*Furniture in pine, walnut, oak, quilts. Primitive
finished pine and original paint.*

Flo Jacobs Antiques
4512 E. State St.
Phone 815/398-3875
Saturday, Sunday & Wednesday 1:30 to 5.
Antiques, collectibles, furniture, smalls.

Peddler's Attic
2609 Charles St.
Phone 815/962-8842
Monday thru Saturday 11 to 4.
Vintage clothing, jewelry, antique glass, furniture.

Vintage Adventure
403 11th Street
Phone 815/227-1892
Tuesday thru Saturday 12:30 to 6.
Vintage clothing, bridal gowns, jewelry, furniture.

New Mill Antiques
6583 11th St. (south side of town)
Phone 815/874-8853
Open 6 days 12 to 5, closed Tuesday.
Two buildings of furniture, glassware, kitchenware.

The Homestead (white barn behind house)
3712 N. Central (corner of Riverside)
Phone 815/962-7498
Tuesday thru Sunday 12 to 5.
*Country furniture, primitives, kitchen
items-you'll like this one.*

Chris' Antiques
5152 Harlem Rd.
Phone 815/654-1610
Monday thru Saturday 11 to 4.
*12 rooms of country items and primitives. Vintage
clothing, lots of buttons, quilts.*

Collin's Antiques
1012 Old Ralston Rd.
Phone 815/633-2875
Mon. thru Fri. 10 to 5, Sat. & Sun. by chance.
*Pine, oak & walnut furniture, primitives.
Kitchen items.*

Rockford *(continued)*

The Eagle's Nest Antiques
7080 Old River Rd. (3 miles N. of Rockford,
1/2 mile off Rt. 2) Phone 815/633-8410
By chance or appt.
Country furniture, rough, refinished, painted.
Stoneware, toys, kitchen items.

OUTDOOR MARKET: 'May 25-26, July 5-6, Aug.
31 & Sept. 1. In the parking lots of Antique Malls I
& II, 5301 & 5411 East State Street. Opens at 8 am.

Machesney Park

Backroads Antique Emporium
4940 Minns Drive
Phone 815/877-4234
Friday 6 to 9, Sat. 10 to 5.
Hall china, depression glass, tea pots, dolls.

Rockton

The Big D's Antiques & Vintage Fashions
110 N. Blackhawk Blvd.
Phone 815/624-6300
Monday thru Saturday 11:30 to 4:30.
Furniture, vintage clothing, toys, McCoy
pottery, clocks & watches, jewelry.

Old & Used Furniture
112 N. Blackhawk Blvd.
Phone 815/624-6300
Monday thru Saturday 11:30 to 4:30.
Furniture, from antique to modern.

Roscoe Floral Cow & Co.
106 W. Main St.
Phone 815/624-2666
Monday thru Saturday 9 to 5.
A floral shop that sells antiques. Specializing
in country, Norwegian, & American Indian. Also
a museum of 18th C. enameled glass.

Nichols Antique Shop
212 W. Main St.
Phone 815/624-4137
Open 7 days, 10 to 5.
General line of antiques. Coins, stamps, books, toys.

See page 177 for Wisconsin listings north of
Rockton, starting with Beloit, Wisconsin.

Pecatonica

Time & Again Antiques Mall
402 Main St.
Phone 815/239-2480
Monday thru Saturday 11 to 5.

Pecatonica *(continued)*

Roberta's Antiques
418 Main St.
Phone 815/239-1023
Tues. thru Sat. 10:30 to 4:30, most Sundays 11 to 4.
Furniture, primitives, kitchenware.

Antiques at Hillwood Farm
498 N. Farwell Bridge Rd.
Phone 815/239-2421
Summer: Wednesday thru Saturday 11 to 5,
Call ahead advised. Winter: by appt.
Shaker and New England furniture.

Ghost Town Antiques
On US 20, between Rockford and Freeport.
Phone 815/239-1188
Open by chance or appointment.
Furniture, primitives, country items, brass, copper.

Seward

Backwoods Antiques
Pecatonica Rd., 3 miles south of Hwy. 20
Phone 815/247-8420
Open 7 days - hours vary.
Toy trucks, World's Fair Items, Roseville, Red Wing.

Leaf River

Corner Antique Shoppe
117 N. Main St.
Phone 815/738-2863
Antiques, collectibles, automobilia.

Freeport

The Swan's Nest
Business Rt. 20 & Bypass 20 West
Phone 815/235-SWAN
7 days 9 to 5, Friday 'til 9.
American country, quilts, decoys, folk art.

Antique Market
in same building as Swan's Nest (above)
7 days 9 to 5, Friday 'til 9.
18 dealers.

Butch's Antiques
330 W. Pleasant St.
Phone 815/233-4437
Monday thru Friday 8:30 to 5.
American country antiques and primitives.

Freeport *(continued)*

Luecke's Antique Mall
10-1/2 E. Main St.
Phone 815/233-0021
Monday thru Saturday 10 to 5, Sun. 12 to 5.
30 dealers in the1892 Blust building.

Main Street Antiques
12 E. Main St.
Phone 815/233-0027
Monday thru Saturday 10 to 5, Fri. 'til 8.
10 dealers.

Eleroy

Treasures of Time Antiques
101 Bridge St.
Phone 815/233-2202
Saturday & Sunday 11 to 5.
Oak and walnut furniture, lamps, quilts in the old stone church built in 1869.

Raccoon Hollow Antiques
7114 Rt. 20 West (5 miles west of Freeport)
Phone 815/233-5110
Everyday 9 to 5.
Country furniture and collectibles.

Lena

Quilted Treasures
209 E. Main St.
Phone 815/369-9104
Quilt shop downstairs, antique quilts upstairs.

Rebecca's Parlor Antiques
208 S. Schuyler St. (Rt. 73, 1 mile north of Rt. 20)
Phone 815/369-4196
Open daily 10 to 5.
Glassware, porcelain, furniture, collectibles.

Wool Gatherings
210 E. Lena St.
Phone 815/369-2330
Old & new spinning wheels and everything related to spinning.

D. J.'s Antiques
326 E. Lena St.
Phone 815/369-4888
Open by chance or appt.
Glassware, furniture, old tools, license plates.

St. Andrews Antiques
12075 W. Oak Street
Phone 815/369-5207
By chance or appt.
Furniture, walnut, pine, original paint, quilts.

Lena *(continued)*

Cubbies Bull Pen
211 N. Schuyler St.
Phone 815/369-2862
Tues. thru Fri. 1 to 6, Sat. 10 to 6, Sun. 1 to 6.
Sports cards, posters, pennants, sports memorabilia.

*See page 178 for Wisconsin towns just north
of the Illinois border.*

Pearl City

Circle H Farm Antiques
65 - Hwy. 73 North
Phone 815/443-2917 By chance or appt.
General line, cast iron and tin toys, farm toys.

Sew Many Antiques
160 S. Main St.
Phone 815/443-2211
Mon. Wed. Fri. 11 to 7, Tues. Thurs. 3:30 to 7,
Sat. 10 to 5, Sun. 11 to 5.
*Antique & quilt shop. Furniture, glassware,
advertising, tools and toys.*

Stockton

Tredegar Antique Market
208 E. North Ave. (Rt. 20)
Phone 815/947-2360
Daily 10 to 5, Fri. & Sun. 'til 6, Wed. 12 to 5.

**Grandpa & Grandma's Antiques &
 Collectibles**
118 W. Front St.
Phone 815/947-2411
Tues. thru Fri. 10 to 5, Sat. 'til 3:30, Sun. 12 to 3,

Warren

Groom Antiques
416 Pearl St.
Phone 815/745-3439
by chance or appointment.
Antique furniture & collectibles.

Thunder Creek Antiques
9178 Cole St.
Phone 815/745-3498
Open by chance, but usually there in summer.
*In the summer kitchen of a brick Victorian home.
Furniture, jewelry, primitives, glassware, advertising.*

Elizabeth

Shop on the Hill
504 S. Main St. (Rt. 20)
Phone 815/858-3815
6 days 10 to 5, closed Wed, Sunday 11 to 5.
First floor of a Victorian home. Furniture, primitives, stoneware.

Welcome Home Antiques
118 N. Main St. (Rt. 20)
Phone 815/858-3450
Monday thru Saturday 9 to 4.
"100% antiques" says the owner.

Main Street Mini Mall
115 N. Main St.
Phone 815/858-3607
5 days 10 to 4:30, closed Tues. Wed.
Winter: closed Tues. Wed. Thurs.
Antiques, furniture, collectibles, salt & peppers.

Galena

A Touch of Banowetz Antiques
117 So. Main St.
Phone 815/777-3370
7 days, 9 to 5.
Galena's largest shop with 6500 sq. feet of American antique furniture, lamps, clocks, china , glassware. Toys and country accessories.

Stillman Valley

Lockwood's Antiques
5669 Hales Corner Rd.
Phone 815/234-8557
Open most days except Saturday-best to call ahead.
Antiques from 1840's to 1920's.

Oregon

South Wing Antique Mall
in Conover Square, 3rd & Franklin St. - 1st floor.
Phone 815/732-4522
Mon. thru Fri. 9:30 to 5:30, Sat. 'til 5, Sun. 11 to 5.
Multi-dealer shop.

Conover Village Antiques
in Conover Square, 3rd & Franklin (upstairs)
Phone 815/732-2134
Mon. thru Fri. 9:30 to 5:30, Sat 'til 5, Sun. 11 to 5.
In a brick building on the Rock River that housed a piano factory from 1893 to 1977.

Oregon *(continued)*

Variety Shoppe Mall
200 N. Third
Phone 815/732-2484
7 days 10 to 5.
Collectibles, gifts, quilts, dolls, antiques.

Silo Antiques
1490 N. Rt. 2 (across from Blackhawk Statue.)
Phone 815/732-4042
7 days, 10 to 5.
Primitives, oak & walnut furniture, elegant
glassware, china, depression glass.

Polo

Trotter Restorations & Antiques, Inc.
115-117 W. Mason St.
Phone 815/946-2592
Monday thru Saturday 9 to 5.
Mall is in a 1901 three story building
that is being restored. Antique light fixtures,
cookstoves, furniture, smalls, hardware.

Dixon

E & M Antique Mall
1602 S. Galena Ave.
Phone 815/288-1900
Monday thru Saturday 10 to 6, Sun. 10 to 5.

Brinton Avenue Antique Mall
725 Brinton Ave.
Phone 815/284-4643

Dixon Antique Station Antique Mall
1220 S. Galena Ave.
Phone 815/284-8890
7 days 10 to 4.

Sterling

American Heritage Antique Center
202 First Avenue
Phone 815/622-3000
Monday thru Saturday 10 to 5, Sun. 12 to 5.
Visit this antique center that features quality
antiques and also has a coffeehouse and eatery.
Sterling is just 3 miles north of I-88.

Rock Falls

Rock River Antique Center
2105 East Rt. 30
Phone 815/625-2556
Monday thru Saturday 10 to 7, Sun. 12 to 5.
Large mall with furniture, glassware, toys,
smalls.

Morrison

Ramey's Old Barn Antiques
115 E. Main St.
Phone 815/772-5677
5 days 10 to 4, closed Thurs. & Sun.
Kathy moved from Aurora and Oswego
to the beautiful Victorian town of Morrison.
Stop in and say hello.

Gallery on Main
112 E. Main St.
Phone 815/772-4725
Mon. Tues. Wed. Fri. 9 to 5, Sat. 9 to 12.
A mix of antiques, framing, birdhouses &
flower arrangements.

Storeroom Antiques
622 Lincolnway East
Phone 815/772-7575
Monday thru Saturday 10 to 5.
A small house shop with antiques, primitives,
linens, quilts, collectibles.

Constantly Stitching N' More
13690 Lincoln Rd.
Phone 815/772-2833
Mon. 12 to 9, Tues. thru Fri. 10 to 6, Sat. 'til 5,
Sunday 12 to 4.
Four rooms of antiques, fabrics, notions.

Savanna

Pulford Opera House Antique Mall
330 Main St. (Rt. 84 Great River Rd.)
Phone 815/273-2661
7 days: Mon. thru Thurs. 10:30 to 5:30,
Fri. Sat. 'til 8, Sun. 11 to 6.
June to Sept: Mon. thru Sat. 9:30 to 8.
120 dealers in this turn-of-the-century
Opera House in downtown Savanna.

J. T. Bradley's
314 Main St. (Rt. 84)
Phone 815/273-4555
Mon. thru Thurs. 10:30 to 5:30, Fri. & Sat. 10:30 to 8,
Sunday 10:30 to 6.
28 dealers. Antique back bars a specialty.

Maquoketa, Iowa

Banowetz Antiques
Hwy. 61 North (1 mile north of Maquoketa)
Phone 319/652-2359
Monday thru Saturday 8 to 6, Sunday 10 to 5.
American Victorian furniture, toys.

Banowetz Antique Mall
Jct. of Hwy 61 & 64
Phone 319/652-2359
Monday thru Saturday 8 to 6, Sunday 10 to 5.
Over 155 dealers in this new mall. Complete line
of furniture, back bars, R.S. Prussia, quilts, etc.

Ron & Carol's Old Depot
600 E. Platt (Hwy. 64)
Phone 319/652-2916 (Eve.)
7 days 10 to 5.

Area 6
SOUTHERN WISCONSIN

In this section: Kenosha, Sturtevant, Racine, Caledonia,
Bristol, Union Grove, Milwaukee, Wauwatosa, West Mil-
waukee, West Allis, Brookfield, Waukesha, Delafield,
Oconomowoc, Hartland, Pewaukee, Lannon, Sussex,
Merton,Menomonee Falls, Germantown, Cedarburg,
Grafton, Port Washington,Rubicon, Wilmot, Lake Geneva,
Springfield, Elkhorn, Delavan, Williams Bay, Walworth,
Clinton, Burlington, Waterford, Beloit, Brodhead, Monroe,
Browntown,Afton, Janesville, Milton, Edgerton, Ft. Atkinson,
Cambridge, Deerfield, Lake Mills, Columbus.

Kenosha, Wisconsin

Apple Lane Antiques
On Hwy. S (Hwy.142) 1-1/2 miles east of I-94,
exit Hwy. 142.
10 miles N. of Illinois state line.
Phone 414/859-2017
Wednesday thru Saturday 10 to 5, Sun. 12 to 5.
Open the 1st Sat. in April thru Dec. 24.
*18th & 19th C. furniture and accessories. Civil
War items. A charming setting for this
country shop, don't miss it.*

Apple Lane Antiques

9730 Burlington Rd. (Hwy. S)

1-1/2 miles east of I-94 on Hwy. S (exit Hwy. 142)
KENOSHA, WISCONSIN 53144 • (414) 859-2017

18th & 19th Century Furniture and Accessories including Civil War items

Hwy. KR (Kenosha-Racine County Line)

APPLE LANE ANTIQUES ★ Hwy. S

N

Hwy. 142

Hwy. 158   Hwy 158

Dairyland Greyhound Park

94   HWY. 31

Hwy. 50   Hwy. 50

FACTORY OUTLET CENTRE

Wis. Tourism Info Center

LAKE MICHIGAN

Wisconsin-Illinois State Line

Wed. thru Sat. 10-5, Sun. 12-5
1st Sat. in April thru Dec. 24th

WRITTEN GUARANTEES
NO CRAFTS
NO REPRODUCTIONS

Harold & Gerrie Thurber
Proprietors

Established 1976

Kenosha *(continued)*

Memory Lane
1942 22nd Ave. (4 miles east of I-94)
Phone 414/551-8452
Tuesday thru Saturday 1 to 5.
Enduring favorites will be found here.

The Cypress Tree
722 50th Street
Phone 414/652-6999
Open 6 days 10:30 to 5, closed Saturday.
Jam packed with a variety of antiques and collectibles.

Tutbury Antiques
724 58th Street
Phone 414/652-3375
Saturday & Sunday 11 to 5.
Antique furniture and lighting.

A Miracle on 58th Street
706 58th Street
Phone 414/652-3132
Open 7 days, 10 to 5.
Filled with antiques, collectibles, antique furniture and lighting.

Sara Jane's Antiques & Collectibles
627 58th St.
Phone 414/657-5588
Weekends 12 to 5.
Pottery, estate items, Bakelite, kitchen items, Victoriana.

Racine Antique Mall II
611 58th Street
Phone 414/605-9818
Saturday & Sunday 11 to 5.
Don't miss their other fine shop, Racine Antique Mall, in Racine, Wisconsin.

Kenosha *(continued)*

Helen's Remember When Antique Mall
5801 Sixth Ave.
Phone 414/652-2280
Monday thru Saturday11 to 5, Sun. 12 to 5.
27 dealers .

Greta's
4906 7th Ave.
Phone 414/658-1077
Tuesday thru Saturday 10 to 5.
*From late 1800s to Art Deco. Art, antiques
and furniture gathered by interior designers.*

Dairyland Antique Mall
I-94 and Hwy. 158 (West side of I-94 on
the frontage Rd.)
Phone 414/857-6802
7 days 9 to 5.
95 dealers in the mall just off the expressway.

Sturtevant, Wisconsin

School Days Mall
9500 Durand Ave. (Hwy. 11)
Phone 414/886-1069
Tuesday thru Saturday10 to 5, Sun. 12 to 5.
*Not a little country school, but a 2 story
building housing a multi-dealer shop and boutiques.*

The Revival Antiques
9410 Durand Ave. (Hwy. 11)
Phone 414/886-3666
Tuesday thru Friday 10 to 2:30, Sat. 11 to 5.
*Enter thru the side door to the English basement.
You'll find a large shop below the church.*

Antique Castle Mall
Hwy. I-94 & 20 (5 blocks south of McDonald's on
the frontage road.) • Phone 414/886-6001
7 days 10 to 5. (Closed Tues. Jan. thru May.)
*You can see the building on the east side of
highway (I-94) A very nice mall - take time to stop.*

RACINE ANTIQUE MALL

Rennaisance Revival bedroom suite in walnut, handcarved and inlaid with Art Nouveau motives of "Four Seasons" by Alphonse Mucha. Austria / Bohemia circa 1900.

FEATURING:
Large selection of highest quality Austrian, German and Czechoslovakian furniture - from Biedermeir to Art Deco.
SPECIALIZING IN:
Czech Art glass, Pottery, Perfume bottles and Jewelry.

We are located in the historic Downtown Districts of Racine and Kenosha.

RACINE	KENOSHA
310 Main Street	611 58th Street
(414) 633-9229	(414) 605-9818
Mon - Sat 11-5	Sat & Sun 11-5

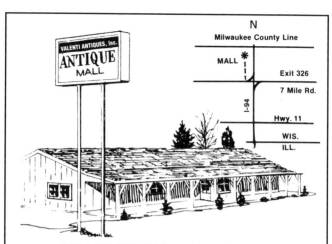

Racine, Wisconsin

Avenue Antiques
1436 Washington Ave. (Rt. 20)
Phone 414/637-6613
Monday thru Saturday 10 to 4:30.
Furniture, glassware, collectibles.

Gifts Now & Then
1408 Washington Ave. (Rt. 20)
Phone 414/634-8883
Mon. thru Sat. 10 to 5, some Sundays.
Many rooms of antiques, teddy bears.

Another Man's Treasures
1354 Washington Ave. (Rt. 20)
Phone 414/633-6869
Monday thru Saturday 10 to 5.
Antiques, collectibles, used furniture.

Ace & Bubba Treasure Hunters
218 6th Street
Phone 414/633-3308
Monday thru Saturday 10 to 5.
Runs the gamut from furniture, bronzes to 50's kitch. Specialty: Royal Doulton - estate, vintage and new.

Koenig's Corner Gallery
300 Main St.
Phone 414/638-1238
Tuesday thru Sunday 10 to 6.
Furniture, jewelry, textiles, fine art, books and, believe it or not, a bicycle rickshaw from Calcutta.

Racine Antique Mall
310 Main St.
Phone 414/633-9229
Monday thru Saturday 11 to 5.
You'll see an extraordinary selection of Czech art glass & perfume bottles and period furniture among other things at this exceptional shop.

Racine *(continued)*

Lee's Flowers & Antiques
1655 N. Main St.
Phone 414/634-3352
Mon. thru Fri. 8 to 6:30, Sat. 'til 5, Sun. 8 to 12.
Antique player pianos, furniture.

Caledonia, Wisconsin

Valenti Antiques, Inc.
On Frontage Rd., west side of I-94,
exit at the "7-mile" exit, then go north.
Phone 414/835-7711
7 days a week, 10 to 5.
Don't pass this by—antiques offered by 30 dealers.

Bristol, Wisconsin

Hawthorn Antiques & Galleries
Hwy. 50, 1-1/2 miles west of I-94,
corner of Hwy. 50 & Country Rd. MB/North.
Phone 414/857-2226
Tuesday thru Sunday 10 to 5.
*Recently opened, they have an ever changing
collection of antiques, furniture and fine art. Housed
in the former Woodworth School, the historic large
red brick building has been meticulously restored.*

Benson Corners Back Door Antique Mall
Hwy. 50, just west of Hwy. 45
Phone 414/857-9456
7 days, 10 to 5.
*Drive down behind the building, park and enter
through the back door - you'll find more than 92
dealer spaces.*

Union Grove, Wisconsin

Storm Hall Antique Mall
835 15th Ave. (Hwy. 45 & 11)
Phone 414/878-1644
Tuesday thru Saturday 11 to 5, Sun. 12 to 5.
Victorian furniture, art pottery, glassware,
on 2 floors.

SHOW: Racine Antiques Fair. Union Grove, Wis.
County Fairgrounds at Rt. 45 & Hwy. 11. June 29,
Aug. 3, Sept. 14, 1997, 8 am to 4 pm.

Milwaukee, Wisconsin

In Downtown Milwaukee:

D & R International Antiques, Ltd.
137 East Wells St. (across from the Pabst Theatre.)
Phone 414/276-9395
Generally open Wednesday thru Saturday 11 to 5.
Monday & Tuesday by appointment.
The most exclusive in 18th & 19th C. antiques.
One of a kind European and American furniture,
clocks, fine art and decorative accessories. Much
of their inventory is of the period.

Milwaukee *(continued)*

Peter Bentz Antiques
771 N. Jefferson
Phone 414/271-8866
By chance or appt.
Small antique shop with silver, jewelry and fine art.

Fifth Avenue Antiques
422 N. Fifth St.
Phone 414/271-3355
Mon. thru Fri. 10 to 6, Sat. 10 to 5, Sun. 12 to 5.
*Furniture—Victorian, mission, primitive &
traditional, lighting, crystal, on 2 floors.*

Centuries Antiques
326 N. Water St.
Phone 414/278-1111
Fri. thru Mon. 11 to 5. In winter: open 6 days,
closed Tuesday.
*Elegant shop featuring fine antiques, furniture,
paintings, glass and more.*

Water Street Antique Market
318 N. Water St.
Phone 414/278-7008
Monday thru Saturday 11 to 5, Sun. 12 to 5.
100 dealers on 3 floors.

Wishful Things
207 E. Buffalo St.
Phone 414/765-1117
Mon. thru Fri. 9 to 5, weekends by chance or appt.
*Specializing in exquisite art glass, this gallery
also has fine porcelain and select smalls.*

Lights of Olde
203 N. Water St.
Phone 414/223-1130
Monday thru Saturday 11 to 5.
Victorian furniture, large and small.

Milwaukee *(continued)*

Milwaukee Antique Center
341 N. Milwaukee St.
Phone 414/276-0605
Mon. thru Fri. 11 to 5, Sat. 10 to 5, Sun. 12 to 5.
This huge building has 2 floors and a basement filled with antiques and collectibles.

Jacquelynn's China Matching Service
219 N. Milwaukee St.
Phone 414/272-8880
Monday thru Friday 8:30 to 5:30, Sat. 10 to 2.
Matching dinnerware, English & American.

Brass Light Gallery
131 South 1st Street
Phone 414/271-8300
Monday thru Friday 10 to 5, Saturday 10 to 4.
Restored antique and reproduction lighting.

Antique Center-Walker's Point
1134 South 1st Street
Phone 414/383-0655
Mon. thru Sat. 10 to 5, closed Tues. Sun. 12 to 5.
Antique dealers on 3 floors.

Milwaukee *(continued)*

Clinton Street Antiques
1110 S. First St.
Phone 414/647-1773
Wednesday thru Sunday 11 to 5.
Primitives, advertising.

Gallery of Antiques
1005 South 60th St.
Phone 414/771-9166 or 800/522-9166
Monday thru Friday 8 to 5, Sat. 10 to 4.
Victorian & oak furniture, period furnishings,
lamps, pottery, fine artwork, decorative accessories.

Wauwatosa, Wisconsin

Echols Antiques & Gifts
6230 W. North Ave.
Phone 414/774-5556
Tuesday thru Friday 10 to 5, Sat. 9 to 3.
Porcelain, fine glassware, collectibles, furniture.

Wauwatosa Antique Gallery
6917 W. North Ave.
Phone 414/453-6829
Mon. thru Fri. 12 to 4:30, Sat. 10 to 3,
Furniture.

West Milwaukee, Wisconsin

Second Chances Antiques & Collectibles
4633 W. National Ave.
Phone 414/645-8066
Wednesday thru Friday 12 to 5, Sat. 10 to 5.

West Allis, Wisconsin

Carol's Antiques & More
7627 W. Greenfield Ave.
Phone 414/476-4744
Open 2 days: Tuesday & Saturday 11 to 4.
Old dolls, china, depression glass, smalls.

Brookfield, Wisconsin

Stonewood Village Antiques
17700 W. Capitol Drive
Phone 414/781-7195
Monday thru Saturday 10 to 5, Sun. 11 to 4:30.
20 dealers fill the 1865 farmhouse.

Waukesha, Wisconsin

A Dickens of a Place Antique Center
521 Wisconsin Ave. (I-94 west to exit 295, south
6 stoplights to St. Paul Ave.)
Phone 414/542-0702
Monday thru Saturday 10 to 5, Sun. 12 to 5.
*30 dealers showing furniture, primitives,
china, glassware, dolls, vintage clothing, etc.*

Fortunate Finds
124 E. St. Paul Ave.
Phone 414/542-8110
Thurs. Fri. 12 to 5, Sat. 10 to 2.
Furniture & accessories from the British Isles.

Kruger's Antiques
401 Madison St.
Phone 414/542-7722
Tuesday thru Friday 12 to 5, Sat. 10 to 5.
*2 floors full, from old square nails to Limoges.
This is their 50th year in business.*

The Heirloom Doll Shop
416 E. Broadway
Phone 414/544-4739
Monday thru Friday 10 to 6, Sat. 'til 5.
Dolls from all eras.

Just a Little Bit Country
N4 W22496 Blue Mound Rd. (Hwy. JJ)
Phone 414/542-8050
Monday thru Saturday 10 to 5:30, Sun. 12 to 5.
*Their specialty is American primitives.
Also see pine cupboards, tables, collectibles.*

Parmelia's Front Porch
Behind "Just a Little Bit Country" listed above.
Phone 414/896-2131
Monday thru Saturday 10 to 5:30, Sun. 12 to 5.
*Furniture & accessories: early New England,
American primitive, farmstead.*

Waukesha, Wisconsin (*continued*)

Brookdale Village
W305 S4095 Brookhill Rd. (Take Hwy. 59 west of
Waukesha to Brookhill Rd. Near Genesee, Wis.
Turn north on Brookhill Rd. to Brookdale Village.)
Phone 414/968-4621 or 414/548-0056
April thru November: Wed. thru Sun. 10 to 4.
*Once the home of world famous Brookhill Dairy
that supplied Milwaukee and Chicago with milk.
They had their own building at the '34 Chicago
World's Fair. Now 4 buildings are open with
antiques, collectibles, furniture and a museum.*

Delafield, Wisconsin

Delafield Antiques Center
803 Genesee St.
Phone 414/646-2746
Mon. thru Sat. 10 to 6, Fri. 'til 8, Sun 12 to 5.
*75 dealers in 18th, 19th and early 20th C.
furniture, accessories, art. This is the one everyone
is talking about. An outstanding mall.*

Celtic Antiques
810 Genesee St.
Phone 414/646-3000 • Call ahead for hours.
*18th & 19th C. Irish country pine and formal
mahogany furniture. Brass, lamps, smalls.*

Delafield, Wisconsin (*continued*)

Red River Furniture
608 Milwaukee St.
Phone 414/646-8010
Monday thru Saturday 10 to 5, Sun. 12 to 4.
*They sell new Amish furniture and gifts, but
are also adding antique furniture to the shop.*

Encore Antiques
630 Milwaukee St.
Phone 414/646-8738
Monday thru Saturday 11 to 5:30, Sun. 1 to 5:30,
Antiques, furniture, glassware.

Rickety Robin Antiques
703 Milwaukee St.
Phone 414/646-8870
Monday thru Saturday 11 to 5,
once in a while on Sunday 1 to 5.
Furniture, wicker, Victoriana, jewelry, glassware.

Oconomowoc, Wisconsin

Marsh Hill Ltd.
456 N. Waterville Rd.
Phone 414/646-2560
May to Christmas: Thurs. thru Sun. 12 to 5,
other times by appointment.
*Cosmopolitan country furniture. Also flow blue,
Staffordshire, candlesticks, etc. in this rural,
picturesque antique shop—don't miss it.*

Hartland, Wisconsin

Blue Willow Antiques
127 E. Capitol Drive
Phone 414/367-7671
Monday thru Saturday 10 to 5, Sun. 12 to 5.
Fine furniture, glassware, primitives, collectibles.

Heartland's Antiques
418 Merton Ave. - #3B
Phone 414/367-9828
Monday thru Saturday 10 to 5, Sun. 11 to 5.

Pewaukee

Old Lynndale Farm
N47 W28270 Lynndale Rd. Hwy. 16 to exit 184
(Jungbluth Rd-KE), north on KE 1 block to JK-then
east 1/2 mile.
Phone 414/369-0350
Mon. thru Fri. 10 to 5:30, Sat. 10 to 4, Sun. 12 to 4.
*2 big barns, 27 dealers with primitives, glassware,
pottery, linens, furniture. Also a craft mall
and tearoom.*

Lannon, Wisconsin

Betti Anne's Antiques
7291 N. Lannon Rd.
Phone 414/255-6750
6 days 11 to 5, closed Tuesday.

Sussex, Wisconsin

Mindy's Antiques
N56 W22053 Silver Spring Rd.
Phone 414/246-3183
Thursday, Friday, Saturday 10 to 4.
18th & early 19th C. furniture and accessories.

Steeple House Antiques
N63 W23811 Main St.
Phone 414/820-0487
Tuesday thru Saturday 11 to 5, Sun. 12 to 4.
Located in a 135 year old building that was formerly a German Lutheran Church.

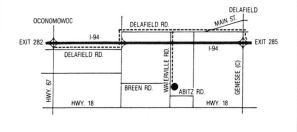

Merton, Wisconsin

The Golden Swan
7148 Main St.
Phone 414/538-1550
Mon. thru Fri. 10 to 5:30, Thurs. 'til 8,
Sat. 10 to 5, Sun. 11 to 4.
Kitchen cupboards, armoires, dry sinks,
seed counters.

Menomonee Falls, Wisconsin

Second Chances Antiques & Collectibles
N86 W16394 Appleton Ave.
Phone 414/251-7989
7 days 10 to 5.
Oak furniture, glassware, mirrors, crocks, etc.

Menomonee Falls Antiques
N88 W16683 Appleton Ave.
Phone 414/250-0816
7 days 10 to 6.
Over 50 dealers, "specialize in inexpensive
collectibles and antiques."

Needful Things, Specialty Gifts, Antiques
& Consignments
N88 W16733 Appleton Ave.
Phone 414/250-1050
Tuesday thru Saturday 10 to 5, Sun. & Mon. 11 to 4.
Have a cup of coffee while you're shopping.

Attic Memories - Collectibles & Antiques
N89 W16776 Appleton Ave.
Phone 414/251-4040
Tuesday thru Saturday 10 to 5, Sun. & Mon. 11 to 4.
A new large mall with approx 70 dealers.

Germantown, Wisconsin

Pilgrim Antique Mall
W156 N11500 Pilgrim Rd.
Phone 414/250-0260
Monday thru Saturday 10 to 5, Sun. 12 to 4.
Furniture, primitives, jewelry, glassware.

Cedarburg, Wisconsin

In Cedar Creek Settlement, N70 W6340
Bridge St, corner of Washington Ave.

Hours for all shops:
Mon thru Sat. 10 to 5, Sun. 11 to 5.

On the 2nd floor:
Dime A Dance
Phone 414/377-5054
Vintage clothing, laces, jewelry,
crocheted bedspreads.

Cedarburg, Wisconsin (*continued*)

Cedar Creek Antiques
Phone 414/377-2204
8 dealer shop.

Spool 'n Spindle Antiques
Phone 414/377-4200
Antique furniture and accessories.

Cedar Creek Settlement, W63 N706
Washington Ave. 1st floor:
The Collectors Gallery
Washington Ave.
Phone 414/375-3340
Antiques, collectibles, estate jewelry.

* * *

Stonemill Antiques
N69 W6333 Bridge Rd.
Phone 414/377-9240
7 days 10 to 5.
Furniture, primitives, toys, tools, advertising, etc.

Cedarburg, Wisconsin *(continued)*

Creekside Antiques
N69 W6335 Bridge Rd.
Phone 414/377-6131
Monday thru Saturday 10 to 5, Sun. 11 to 4.
Lower level but windows are at creekside. 12 dealers.

Nouveau Antique & Jewelry Parlor
W62 N594 Washington Ave.
Phone 414/375-4568
Monday thru Saturday 10 to 5, Sun. 12 to 5.
Glassware, jewelry, Victorian furniture in
the purple "painted lady."

Patricia Frances Interiors -
The Consignment Store
W62 N634 Washington Ave.
Phone 414/377-7710
Monday thru Saturday 11 to 5.
Delightful collection of antiques on consignment.
3 rooms downstairs, 2 rooms upstairs.

Crow's Nest
N66 W6404 Cleveland St.
Phone 414/377-3039
Open most of the time, but best to call ahead.
Fine china, tin, brass with a country English flair.

Heritage Lighting
W62 N572 Washington Ave.
Phone 414/377-9033
Monday thru Saturday 10:30 to 4:30, Sun. 11 to 4.
Specializing in antique gas & electric fixtures.
Chandeliers, sconces, table & floor lamps.

American Country Antiques
W61 N506 Washington Ave.
Phone 414/375-4140
Tuesday thru Saturday 11 to 5.
18th & 19th C. period and American country
furniture and accessories. On the south
end of Washington Ave. A very nice shop.

Don's Resale & Antiques
N57 W6170 Portland Rd.
Phone 414/377-6868
5 days 10 to 5, closed Tuesday & Sunday.
In the Old Mill.

Grafton, Wisconsin

Grafton Antique Mall
994 Ulao Rd. (Interstate 43 at Hwy 60 - exit 92,
then 1 block east.
Phone 414/376-0036
7 days 10 to 5, extended hours in summer.
The mall is set back from the road. Meander through
this a-mazeing shop where every twist and turn
discloses another treasure filled room.

Grafton Antique Mall

ART • CLOCKS • COLLECTIBLES
COUNTRY • DEPRESSION GLASS
VINTAGE JEWELRY • PAINTINGS
POTTERY • VICTORIAN • OAK • DECOYS
PRIMITIVES • CHINA • CROCKS
HUNTING & FISHING ITEMS
LINENS • BOOKS • COINS • TOYS
FURNITURE
displayed in vignette room settings

Open10 TO 5 Daily
call for extended summer hours
Master Card • Visa • Discover
American Express

I-43
★ GRAFTON
   ANTIQUE
   MALL
Cedarburg
Exit
92
● Milwaukee
N ↑
I-94

I-43 & Hwy. 60
Exit 92, east I block
(EZ off - EZ on)
Grafton, Wisconsin 53024

414-376-0036

Port Washington

Port Antiques
314 N. Franklin (downtown)
Phone 414/284-5520
7 days 10 to 5, Fri. 'til 7.
*Country, Victorian, primitives. Furniture,
glassware, vintage clothing, toys, tools, decoys.*

Gordon's
2275 N. Port Washington Rd. (Hwy. 32)
(1-1/2 miles South of Port Washingon)
Phone 414/377-4313
7 days 10 to 5.
Victorian, American Indian, postcards.

Rubicon, Wisconsin

Nancy Aldrich Antiques
N1455 Hwy. P. 4 miles North of Mapleton
on Dodge City Hwy. P. Log house just north
of Washington Rd.
Phone 414/474-4593
Open by chance or appointment.
*From furniture to papier mache to regional
Wisconsin items - a shop that's
something special.*

❧ ❧ ❧

Just north of the Illinois border:

Wilmot, Wisconsin

Mary's on Main
Main Street, between the postoffice and
Phillips 66 gas station.
Phone 414/862-9694 or 414/862-2234
Saturday 10 to 4:30, Sunday 12 to 4:30, or call her
for an appointment.
*Seven rooms of furniture, crystal, lamps,
jewelry and more. Shenandoah design collectibles.*

Wilmot, Wisconsin *(continued)*

The Country Cottage
Fox River Rd. & 112th Street • Phone 414/862-9833
Open May thru Nov: Fri. 11 to 4, Sat. 10 to 5,
Sun. 12 to 4:30.
Antiques, collectibles, gifts in the old greenhouse.

Lake Geneva, Wisconsin

Lake Geneva Antique Mall
829 Williams St. (8 blocks north of Main St. on
Hwy. 120.) • Phone 414/248-6345
7 days 10 to 5, Fridays 'til 8.
*50 dealers showing a variety of interesting
antiques. You'll find many treasures here.*

The Steffen Collection
611 Main St. (Hwy 50) • Phone 414/248-1800
Monday thru Saturday10 to 5, Sun. 12 to 5.
*Large shop (9 showrooms) filled with antique
furniture and accessories.*

Sign of the Unicorn
233 Center St. (1/2 block north of Main)
Phone 414/248-1141
Monday thru Saturday 10 to 5, Sun. 12 to 5.
Antique prints: botanicals, architecturals, old maps.

Springfield, Wisconsin

Springfield Salvage
7242 Spring St. (on Hwy. 120 & 36)
Phone 414/248-4076
Saturday & Sunday 12 to 5.
Architectural antiques from Chicago and Milwaukee mansions—mantels, doors, lighting, etc.

Elkhorn, Wisconsin

Powell's Antique Shop
14 W. Geneva St.
Phone 414/723-2952
Wednesday thru Sunday, open qt 10.
Kerosene lamps, furniture, glassware.

Heirlooms
12 S. Wisconsin
Phone 414/723-4070
Monday thru Saturday 10:30 to 5.
General line and some items crafted from antiques.

Van Dyke's Antiques
20 S. Wisconsin St.
Phone 414/723-4909
Monday thru Saturday 10 to 5.
Oak furniture a specialty.

Past to Present Consignment Shop
23 S. Wisconsin St.
Phone 414/723-2933
Monday thru Saturday 12 to 5.
Antiques, vintage glassware, etc.

Bits of Past & Present
5691 Hwy. 11
Phone 414/723-4763
Tuesday thru Saturday 10 to 5.
General line, Victoriana, country.

Elkhorn, Wisconsin *(continued)*

Twin Pines Antique Mall
5438 Hwy. 11, 1/2 mile west of Elkhorn
Phone 414/723-4492
Tuesday thru Sunday 10 to 5.
14 dealers.

❋ ❋ ❋

Delavan, Wisconsin

Delavan Antique & Art Centre
230 E. Walworth Ave.
Phone 414/740-1400
Mon. thru Thurs. 11 to 6, Fri. & Sat. 11 to 8,
Sun. 12 to 5.
Exciting new antique centre in the old
Schultz Bros Five and Dime building with
floor to ceiling windows. Now it is brimming with
the choice selections of 75 antique dealers.

3 Rings Antiques in Beall Jewelers
305 E. Walworth Ave.
Phone 414/728-8577
Mon. thru Sat. 9 to 5:30, Thurs. & Fri. 'til 8.
Antique and estate jewelry, glassware, collectibles,
old watches and clocks.

Delavan, Wisconsin *(continued)*

Antiques of Delavan
229 E. Walworth Ave.
Phone 414/728-9977
Monday thru Saturday 10 to 5, Sun. 12 to 3.
Antiques, crafts and collectibles, including furniture, glassware, dolls, linens, jewelry.

Williams Bay

Bay Salvage
84 Geneva St. (across from Charlie O's)
Saturday & Sunday 12 to 5.
Architectural artifacts, furniture, stained glass, etc.

Walworth, Wisconsin

Parlor & Pantry
400 Kenosha St. (Rt. 67), a few blocks east
of the stoplight.)
Phone 414/275-6016
Mon. thru Sat. 10 to 5, closed Tues., Sun. 12 to 5.
Winter: open 'til 4:30.
Antiques beautifully displayed in an 8 room Victorian house.

The Grapevine Shop - Craft,
Antique & Retail Mall
325 Kenosha St.
Phone 414/275-2511
Mon. thru Fri. 10 to 7, Sat. 10 to 6, Sun. 12 to 5.
Just opening, has a few antique dealers.

American Pioneer Antiques
108 Madison St. (on the square)
Phone 414/275-9696
Thurs. Fri. Sat. 10:30 to 5, Sun. 12 to 5.
Ingrid Suppes shop on the square features primitives, quilts, high country furniture.

Walworth, Wisconsin *(continued)*

Bittersweet Farm & High Button Shoes
114 Madison St. (on the square)
Phone 414/275-3062
Mon. thru Sat. 10 to 4, Sun. 12 to 4, hours may
vary in winter.
General line, books & prints, lamps.

On the Square Antique Mall
Hwy 14 & 67 (west side of the square.)
Phone 414/275-9858
Monday thru Saturday 10 to 5, Sun. 11 to 5.
A supermarket size shop with 90 dealers.

Raggedy An-tiques
216 S. Main St.
Phone 414/275-5866
Summer: Daily 10:30 to 5, closed Tues. & Wed.
Sun. 12 to 5. Winter (Jan. thru May 1st.):
Fri. Sat. Mon. 10:30 to 4:30, Sun. 12 to 4:30.
Furniture, primitives, dolls, toys, books.

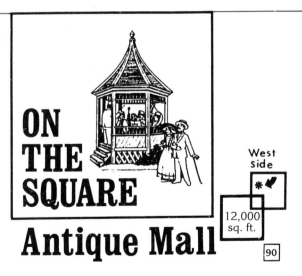

Walworth, Wisconsin *(continued)*

Van's Antiques
Hwy. 14, north of Walworth, near the
Hwy. O intersection.
Phone 414/275-2773
Tues. thru Fri. 1 to 5, Sat. & Sun. 10 to 5.
Shop is kept in apple pie order.

Clinton, Wisconsin

Studio B
223 Allen St.• Phone 608/676-5392
Thursday thru Sunday 12 to 5.
Furniture, vintage radios and cameras and
lots of other things including architectural items.

Nana's House of Antiques & Collectibles
244 Allen St.
Phone 608/676-5535
Monday thru Saturday 10 to 4, Sun. 11 to 4.
35 dealers in downtown Clinton shop.

Smokehouse Antique Mall
402 Front St.
Phone 608/676-2251
Monday. thru Saturday 10 to 4, Sun. 12 to 4.
20 dealers.

Burlington, Wisconsin

Antique Alley
481 Milwaukee Ave. (Hwy. 36) 10 miles east of
Lake Geneva.
Phone 414/763-5257
Monday thru Saturday 10 to 5, Sun. 12 to 5.
Forty dealers have pitchers, pine, prints, etc.

Burlington, Wisconsin *(continued)*

Gingham Dog Antiques
109 & 120 E. Chestnut St.
Phone 414/763-4759
Mon. thru Sat. 10 to 5 when not doing shows.
Country, walnut, Victorian, oak furniture.

Waterford, Wisconsin

Freddy Bear's Antique Mall
2819 Beck Drive (just off Hwy. 36 at Hwy. 20 West)
Phone 414/534-BEAR
7 days, 9:30 to 5.
*Furniture, glassware, primitives, jewelry,
baseball cards.*

Heavenly Haven Antique Mall and Divine Shoppes
318 W. Main St.
Phone 414/534-4400 • 7 days 9:30 to 5.
*Glassware, furniture, primitives, collectibles,
new and used books and a coffee shop.*

Dover Pond Antiques
28016 Washington Ave. (Hwy. 20, 1/2 mile
east of Hwy. 36.) Phone 414/534-6543
Fri. thru Mon. 11 to 5. Best to call ahead.
In winter: weekends or by appt.
In a 102 year old timbered ceiling stone barn.

✳ ✳ ✳

Beloit, Wisconsin

Rindfleisch Antiques
520 E. Grand Ave.
Phone 608/365-1638
Monday thru Saturday 10 to 5.
*Two floors of furniture, glassware, fine
china, Indian artifacts, architectural items.*

Beloit, Wisconsin *(continued)*

Brass Town Antiques
810 E. Grand Ave.
Phone 608/362-6409
Friday & Saturday 12 to 5.
Mission period art, jewelry, furniture in a small
Victorian cottage originally built for the Beloit brass
workers.

The Nest Egg
816 E. Grand Ave.
Phone 608/365-0700
Monday thru Friday 10 to 5, Sat. 10 to 4.
Antique jewelry, glass & china, furniture.

Riverfront Antique Mall
306 State St.
Phone 608/362-7368
Mon. thru Fri. 9 to 5, Sat. 'til 4, Sun. 12 to 4.
20 dealers.

Caple Country Antiques
309 State St.
Phone 608-362-5688
Mon. thru Fri. 10 to 5, Sat. 10 to 4.
Specializing in oak furniture, large pieces. Also
lamps, glassware, linens, etc.

WEST OF BELOIT

Brodhead, Wisconsin

Brodhead Antique Mall
1027 First Cedar Ave.
Phone 608/897-2696
Mon. Tues 10 to 5, Wed. thru Sat. 9 to 5, Sun. 12 to 5.
3 floors featuring 30 dealers.

Monroe, Wisconsin

New Moon Antiques
1606 11th Street (on the square)
Phone 608/325-9100
Monday thru Friday 9 to 5, Sat. 10 to 4.
Furniture, glassware, coins.

Garden Gate Floral & Antiques
1717 11th St.
Phone 608/329-4900 & 1-800-701-4985
Monday thru Saturday 8:30 to 5:30.
In half of the large (former) Maicos Supper Club
you'll find furniture, including cupboards, in
oak, walnut, pine, cherry. The other half is floral.

Monroe, Wisconsin *(continued)*

Monroe Antiques & Collectible Mall
1003 16th Ave.
Phone 608/328-8000
New mall opening in mid-April.

It's A Bunch of Crock/Breezy Acres
1027 16th Ave.
Phone 608/328-1444
Monday thru Saturday 9 to 4, Sun. 10 to 4.
Breezy Acres is located behind "It's A Bunch."

Bev's Attic Treasures
1018-1/2 17th Ave. (above Wolf's Office Supply)
Phone 608/325-6200
Open Fridays 10 to 5.
The shop includes a Star Wars Museum and other displays.

Between Monroe & Browntown, Wisconsin

Cadiz Hills Antiques at the campground.
W7542 Hwy. 11.
Phone 608/966-3310
By appt. in winter, opens in mid-March.

Browntown, Wisconsin (pop. 236)

The Mill Street Antique General Store
102 S. Mill St. (off Hwy. 11)
Phone 608/966-32509
End of April thru October: 6 days
10 am to 9 pm, Sundays by chance.
They sell everything. Leave the highway for one stop shopping: old books and butter, juice and old jewelry. Also on display are several collections of the owner.

Afton

The Country Lady Antiques
5316 Afton Rd.
Phone 608/752-8066
Thursday thru Saturday 10 to 5, Sun. 12 to 4.
Primitives, cupboards, trunks in the old general store building.

Between Janesville & Beloit

Yesterday's Memories Antique Mall
4904 Hwy. 51 - South (at the corner next to Rock Co. Airport)
Phone 608/754-2906
Mondau thru Saturday 10 to 5, Sun. 12 to 5.
20 dealers.

Janesville, Wisconsin

The General Antique Store
On Hwy. 14 & 11 in Emerald Grove.
Phone 608/756-1812
7 days, 1 to 5.
Several rooms of furniture, glass, advertising signs — be sure to stop.

Pipsqueak & Me
220 W. Milwaukee St.
Phone 608/756-1752, 800-964-6488
Monday thru Saturday 10 to 5.
Fine pre-1860's era furniture in cherry, walnut, pine.

Franklin Stove Antiques
301 W. Milwaukee St.
Phone 608/756-5792
Monday thru Saturday 10 to 5.
Refinished furniture, collectibles.

Milton, Wisconsin

Campus Antiques Mall
609 Campus St.
Phone 608/868-3324
Monday thru Saturday 10 to 5, Sun. 12 to 5.
Large mall in the gym of (former) Milton College.

Goodrich Hall Antiques
501 College St.
Phone 608/868-2470
Tuesday thru Saturday 10 to 5, Sun. 12 to 5.
The newest shop in town opening this spring.

Whitford Hall
525 College St.
Phone 608/868-4939
Monday thru Saturday 10 to 5, Sun. 12 to 5.
3 floors of antiques & collectibles.

Milton, Wisconsin *(continued)*

Milton Collectibles Mall
209 Parkview Ave.
Phone 608/868-7595
Monday thru Saturday 10 to 5, Sun. 12 to 5.
20 dealers. Character collectibles, furniture, etc.

Edgerton, Wisconsin

Stone Manor Antiques
42 Hwy. 59, 1 mile west off I-90.
Phone 608/884-8308
Open everyday 9:30 to 5, when not at auctions or
estate sales. *In the barn behind the house is furniture, jewelry, military items.*

Nine R's Antiques
202 S. Main St.
Phone 608/884-4710
Friday, Saturday, Sunday, 10 to 5.
Glass: Carnival, depression, Fenton, etc. Dolls.

Antique and Art Gallery
104 W. Fulton St.
Phone 608/884-6787
Open 6 days, 10 to 5, closed Tuesday.
Furniture, restored brass lighting, glassware.

Edgerton, Wisconsin *(continued)*

Edgerton Resale Mall
204 W. Fulton St.
Phone 608/884-8148
Monday thru Saturday 10 to 5, Sun. 12 to 5.
38 dealers on 3 floors in the 1857
mercantile store.

Mildred's Antiques
4 Burdick St.
Phone 608/884-3031 or 608/884-8718
Monday thru Saturday 9 to 5.
Mildred has been in business 40 years and
says she has furniture, postcards, china, art
glass, "no collectibles."

Pete's Ghost
11947 Dallman Rd. (Take Fulton St. (Hwy. 59)
west. Dallman is the 1st crossroad on the outskirts
of town. Turn north, go about 1 mile.
Phone 608/884-9508
Tuesday thru Saturday 9 to 5.
Primitives, cupboards.

Fort Atkinson

The Antiques Exchange Mall
232 S. Main St.
Phone 414/563-8500
7 days 10 to 5.
15 dealers.

Cambridge, Wisconsin

Cambridge Antique Mall
109 N. Spring St.
Phone 608/423-9952
Open 7 days, 10 to 5:30.
"Coffee's always on" in the 102-year old renovated
church, now home to 25 dealers.

Deerfield, Wisconsin

Old Deerfield Antiques
37 N. Main St. (Hwy. 73, downtown)
Phone 608/764-5743
Monday thru Saturday 10 to 5, Sun. 11 to 4.
Over 40 dealers.

Lake Mills, Wisconsin

Opera Hall Antique Center
211 N. Main St.
Phone 414/648-5026
7 days 10 to 5.
On 3 floors with furniture, tools jewelry, etc.

Lake Mills, Wisconsin *(continued)*

Old Mills Market
109 N. Main St.
Phone 414/648-3030
7 days 10 to 5, in winter closed Tuesdays.
Antiques, furniture, collectibles, crafts.

Columbus, Wisconsin

Kurth Mansion
902 Park Ave.
Phone 414/623-3930
Mon. thru Sat. 10 to 4, closed Tuesday,
Sunday 12 to 4.
1850 to 1930s antiques displayed in the historic
Kurth Mansion built by the founder of a local
brewery. $1.00 admission.

Antique Shoppes of Columbus Mall Annex
141 W. James St. (Hwy. 16)
Phone 414/623-2669
Monday thru Saturday 10 to 4:30, Sun. 12 to 5.
3 floors of lighting & custom shades, vintage
clothing, and a complete lamp restoration shops.

Charisma Antiques
118 S. Ludington (1/2 block south of downtown
stoplight)
Phone 414/623-0317
Monday thru Saturday 10 to 4, Sun. 12 to 4.
Victorian furniture.

Columbus Antique Mall and Museum
239 Whitney St.
Phone 414/623-1992
Open 7 days, 8:30 to 4.
Large mall with over 160 dealers includes a
museum with an extensive display of the 1893
Columbian Exposition a.k.a. the Chicago
World's Fair.

THE VILLAGE GREEN ANTIQUE MALL

Come visit the friendliest antique mall in the Chicagoland area. We offer professional (non dealer) sales assistance and our unique *"guaranteed antique policy."*

16,000 sq. ft. and 60 dealers featuring the best in toys, lighting, glassware, primitives and furniture. We have specialty dealers in art glass, cookbooks, kerosene lamps and 50's collectibles.

We hold a monthly outside antique show the first Sunday of every month, May thru October (except it will be held on the second Sunday in June (the 8th) and the second Sunday in July (the 13th.) These one day shows are open for any dealer or consigner.

A special feature is our "star" room where all 2,000 sq. ft. of merchandise is on sale at 10% to 25% off regular prices.

The Village Green Antique Mall

404 E. North Ave.
(3/4 mile east of Rt. 355)
Lombard, IL 60148
(630) 268-0086

Open Mon-Sat. 10:00 to 5:00, Fri. 'til 9:00 & Sun. 11:00 to 4:00

184

Area 7
WESTERN SUBURBS

In this section: Northlake, Elmhurst, Villa Park, Lombard, Glen Ellyn, Wheaton, St. Charles, Geneva, Batavia, Maple Park, Sycamore, DeKalb, Esmond.

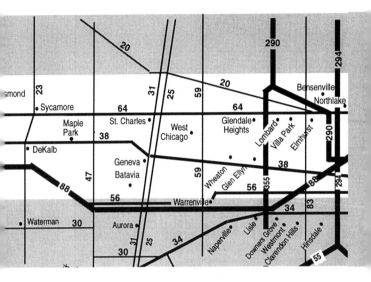

Northlake

Cupid's Antiques
232 E. North Ave. (North side of North Ave. between Roy & Roberta on the service lane.)
Phone (708) 531-0333
Tues. Thurs. Fri. Sat. 10 to 5, Sun. 12 to 5, closed Monday & Wednesday.
Furniture, linens, glassware.

Elmhurst

Circa Antiques & Collectibles
549 Spring Rd.
Phone (630) 834-4088
Tuesday thru Saturday 10 to 5.
Specializing in vintage jewelry, sterling, toys, Czechoslovakian art glass & pottery.

Furniture Arcade
111 W. First St.
Phone (630) 834-8110
Mon. thru Fri. 10 to 5:30, Thurs. 'til 7, Saturday 'til 5.
Furniture from the 20s 30s & 40s, antiques and collectibles.

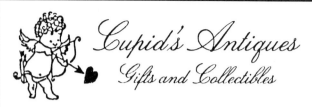
Elmhurst *(continued)*

Elm Classic Consignment
114 W. 3rd St.
Phone (630) 832-8187
Tues. thru Fri. 12 to 6, Thurs. 'til 8,
Saturday 11 to 5.
Consignment 50s, 60s clothing, jewelry, sterling.

'Tiques & Treasures
1001 Riverside Drive
Phone (630) 833-8665
Open only 3 long weekends a year: Memorial Day,
4th of July & Labor Day. Hours are Friday thru
Monday 8 to 3, rain or shine.

Villa Park

Astorville Antiques
51 S. Villa Ave.
Phone (630) 279-5311
Wednesday thru Friday 12 to 5, Sat. 11 to 4.
*Beautifully restored turn of the century oak
and Victorian walnut furniture. Linens & accessories.*

Memories from the Attic
119 S. Villa Ave.
Phone (630) 941-1517
7 days 10 to 5. Closed Fri. morning in summer.
Wedgwood, bronzes, Coca-Cola memoribilia.

Lombard

The Village Green Antique Mall of Lombard
404 E. North Ave. (3/4 mile east of Rt. 355)
Phone (630) 268-0086
7 days: Mon. thru Sat. 10 to 5, Fri. 'til 9, Sun. 11 to 4.
*60 dealers with antiques and collectibles. Also see their
large stock of new reference books about antiques.
Their ad gives details about their once a month (Sunday)
outdoor antique show—held May thru October.*

Lombard *(continued)*

Kohler's Trading Post
638 E. St. Charles Rd.
Phone (630) 620-1220
Tuesday thru Saturday 10 to 5.
Don't dress up.

The Antique Cellar
5 S. Park Ave.
Phone (630) 629-9171
Monday thru Saturday 1 to 5.
The original "cellar" moved to the 1st floor.

Chez Les Antiques
722 S. Main St.
Phone (630) 495-1459
Tues. thru Sat. 11 to 5, Thurs. 'til 9, Sun. 11 to 4.
Glassware, furniture, fine china, etc.

Glen Ellyn

Royal Vale View Antiques (The Barn)
388 Pennsylvania Ave.
Phone (630) 790-3135
Saturdays or by appt.
Architectural, furniture and accessories.

Glen Ellyn *(continued)*

*In the "Little Shops," corner of
Crescent Blvd. and Main St.:*

Patricia Lacock Antiques
526 Crescent Blvd.
Phone (630) 858-2323
Monday thru Saturday 10:30 to 4:30.
*A charming shop filled with jewelry, pressed
and cut glass, china - you'll like it.*

Stagecoach Antiques
526 Crescent Blvd.
Phone (630) 469-0490
Open Monday thru Saturday 11 to 5.
*Antique heirloom jewelry, new designer
jewelry, glassware, china and silver.*

Marcia Crosby - A Gallery
477 Forest Ave.
Phone (630) 858-5665
Mon., Thurs., Fri. & Sat. 10 to 5.
*American historical prints, antique maps,
country antiques.*

The Sign of the Whale Antiques
558 Crescent Blvd.
Phone (630) 469-5320
Monday thru Saturday 10 to 5, Thurs. 'til 8.
*American country furniture, lamps, quilts, folk art,
old baskets and brass.*

Pennsylvania Place
535 Pennsylvania Ave.
Phone (630) 858-1515
Monday thru Saturday 10 to 5, Thurs. 'til 9,
Sunday 12 to 4:30.
*This shop, with many dealers, offers a wide
variety of antiques and collectibles.*

Demise of Glass Companies
listed in the order of their closing

Boston & Sandwich 1825-1888
Greentown 1894-1903
Duncan & Miller 1900-1955
Heisey 1896-1957

Cambridge, Ohio 1901-1958
Westmoreland 1890-1984
Imperial 1904-1985
Fostoria 1887-1986

Many of these former glass companies "live on" in beautiful museums. Old molds have been sold and repros made from them by other companies for many years. If collecting, do your homework!

Wheaton

Wheaton Antique Mall
1621 N. Main St.
Phone (630) 653-7400
Mon. thru Sat. 10 to 5, Thurs. 'til 8, Sun. 12 to 4.
Ask about their 3 other shops in the area.

Gabriel's Trumpet
229 Rice Lake Square (on Butterfield Rd. just east
of Naperville Rd.
Mon. thru Sat. 10 to 5, Thurs. & Fri. 'til 8,
Sunday 12 to 4.
*This 2nd location for the superb Naperville consign-
ment shop will open May 15th.*

SHOW: Antique & Collectible Market
DuPage County Fairground - Rt. 38 or Rt. 64
7 am to 4 pm. 3rd Sunday of each
month (No show in July) Home of the
 ALL NIGHT FLEA MARKET, Aug. 23 & 24, 1997.

St. Charles

Shrivenhan Antique Co.
125 N. 11th Ave.
Phone (630) 584-5843
Friday, Saturday, Sunday 11 to 5.
Importers of fine European antiques.

St. Charles Antiques Shoppe
113 E. Main St.
Phone (630) 443-7414
Tuesday thru Saturday 10 to 5, Sun. 12 to 5.
Antiques, collectibles and home decor.

In historic Century Corners
—just east of the river and north of Main St.

Studio Posh
17 N. 2nd Ave.
Phone (630) 443-0227
Tuesday thru Saturday 10 to 5.
*Garden and architectural items, fabric covered
dress forms, vintage pillows, china.*

Stone House Shops
20 N. 2nd Ave.
Phone (630) 377-6406
Tuesday thru Saturday 10 to 5, Mon. call first.
*4 shops featuring vintage fabrics, laces, trims,
hand painted vintage furniture, jewelry, etc.*

Scentimental Gardens
115 Cedar Ave.
Phone (630) 443-9980
Monday thru Saturday 10 to 5.
*Garden and home interior store. antiques, architec-
tural items, new furniture, new & old gardening
accessories*

Antique Markets I II & III

ST. CHARLES, ILLINOIS
(35 miles west of downtown Chicago)

Visit three of the most complete and outstanding complexes in the Midwest!

Select from...

Glassware - Art to Depression
China - Pottery to Porcelain
Furniture - Country to Formal
Metalware - Tin to Sterling
Jewelry - Celluloid to Platinum

Also... Art Deco, primitives, books and ephemera, prints and paintings, rugs, dolls and toys, linens, quilts and textiles, tools, vintage clothing and collectibles.

Over eighty dealers welcome you to a collectors' cornucopia in three locations!

OPEN 7 DAYS A WEEK, 10 A.M. - 5 P.M.
(Open most holidays)
♦ *Kane Weekend-* I & III Open Fri.& Sat. 8 P.M., II Flexible ♦

ANTIQUE MARKET I - 11 N. Third St., **(630)377-1868**

ANTIQUE MARKET II - 301-303 W. Main St. (Rt. 64)
(630)377-5798 (1st level west),**(630)377-5818** (1st level east)
(630)377-5676 (Upper level)   (Zip Code 60174)

ANTIQUE MARKET III - 413 W. Main St. **(630)377-5599**

♦ Gift certificates available. Layaways. VISA & Mastercard accepted. ♦

192

St. Charles *(continued)*

Pariscope
116 Cedar Ave.
Phone (630) 513-8979
Wednesday thru Saturday 10 to 5.
Furniture, lighting, garden accessories and the
unusual straight from the Paris Flea Market.

Cottage Interiors
210 Cedar Ave.
Phone (630) 377-6844
Tuesday thru Saturday 10 to 5.
Primitives and pine cupboards, furniture,
armoires, tables.

Consigntiques
214 W. Main St.
Phone (630) 584-7535
Monday thru Saturday 10 to 5, Sun. 12 to 4.
Furniture, glassware, collectibles all on consignment.

Brown Beaver Antiques
219 W. Main St.
Phone (630) 443-9430
Tuesday thru Saturday 11 to 5.
Over 100 brass or iron turn of the century beds.
Also bird cages, hall trees, furniture, etc.

The Market
12 N. 3rd St.
Phone (630) 584-3899
Mon. thru Fri. 10 to 5:30, Thurs. 'til 8,
Sat. 10 to 5, Sun. 11 to 5.
This has always been an interesting shop with many
boutiques. Now they also have eight antique dealers.

The Memory Merchant
15 S. Third St.
Phone (630) 513-0340
Open 7 days, 10 to 5.
8 dealers in an older home with primitives,
clocks, furniture, kitchen collectibles.

Riverside Antiques
410 So. First St. (west side of the river,
a few blocks south of Main St.)
Phone (630) 377-7730
7 days: Mon. thru Fri. 10 to 9, Sat. 10 to 6,
Sunday 11 to 5.
Escalators will take you to the 3rd floor - the
antiques are in a wing of the old piano factory.
There are factory outlet shops in the rest of this
large building.

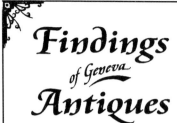

St. Charles (continued)

Antique Market I
11 N. Third St.
Phone (630) 377-1868
Open 7 days, 10 to 5 and most holidays, Fri. &
Sat 'til 8 on Kane County Flea Market weekends.
*Antiques, furniture and collectibles. something
for everyone.*

Antique Market II
301-303 W. Main St. (Rt. 64)
Phone (630) 377-5798 first level west;
(630) 377-5818 first level east;
(630) 377-5676 upper level.
Open 7 days, 10 to 5 and most holidays, Fri. &
Sat 'til 8 on Kane County Flea Market weekends.
*An antique center on 3 levels with lots of
rooms, nooks and crannies filled with antiques.*

Antique Market III
413 W. Main St. (Rt. 64)
Phone (630) 377-5599
Open 7 days, 10 to 5 and most holidays, Fri. &
Sat 'til 8 on Kane County Flea Market weekends.
Jewelry, glass, railroadiana, coins, advertising, etc.

SHOW: Kane County Flea Market
Kane County Fairground, Randall Rd.
1st Sunday of each month. However it opens the
preceding afternoon.
Saturday 1 to 5 pm, Sunday 7 am to 4 pm.

Geneva

A Step in the Past Antiques & Collectibles
122 Hamilton St. (1 block north of State St.)
Phone (630) 232-1611
Tuesday thru Saturday 11 to 5, Sunday 12 to 4.
Nine rooms of furniture, glassware, vintage clothing.

Bill Kohanek Antiques and Decorations
121 W. State St. (Rt. 38)
Phone (630) 232-0552
Tuesday thru Saturday 11 to 5, Sun. by chance.
Formal and country furniture, paintings / prints.

Findings of Geneva Antiques
307 W. State St. (Rt. 38)
3 doors west of 3rd Street
Phone (630) 262-0959
Tuesday thru Saturday 10:30 to 6, Sun. 12 to 5,
extended hours on Kane County weekend.
Vintage linens, cookbooks, Flow Blue, toys, etc.

The Country Store
28 James St. (Rt. 31, 1 blk. S. of Rt. 38)
Phone (630) 232-0335
Monday thru Saturday 9:30 to 5, Sun.12 to 4.
Primitives.

GENEVA *(continued)*

Circa
123 S. Third St.
Phone (630) 208-0013
Monday thru Saturday 11 to 5, Sun. 1 to 5.
Garden antiques and home accessories.

Geneva Antiques Ltd.
220 S. Third St.
Phone (630) 208-7952
Monday thru Saturday 10 to 5, Sun. 12 to 4.
5 rooms of furniture, jewelry, vintage tools, books.

Geneva Antique Market
227 S. Third St., in the Berry House.
Phone (630) 208-1150
Monday thru Saturday 10 to 5, Sunday 12 to 5.
*Furniture, primitives, art pottery, quilts,
linens, toys.*

The Old Jewelry Shop
227 S. Third St., in the Berry House.
Phone (630) 262-8889
Wednesday thru Saturday 10 to 4.
This shop was in Highland Park many, many years.

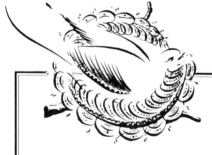

GENEVA *(continued)*

Richard J. Matson Jewelers
312 S. Third St.
Phone (630) 232-4500
Monday thru Saturday 10 to 5.
Jewelry: Deco, nouveau, sterling, Victorian.
cameos, pocket watches and new jewelry.

The Little Traveler
404 S. Third St.
Phone (630) 232-4200
Monday thru Friday 9:30 to 5, Sat. 'til 5:30.
Meander thru the 36 room Victorian mansion to
find English furniture, silver and lots of smalls.
Also enjoy the beautiful boutiques and restaurants.

Fourth Street Galleries
327 Franklin St.
Phone (630) 208-4610
Tuesday thru Saturday 10 to 4.
The 1856 house is filled with antiques, paintings
and prints. Also works by contemporary area artists.
You're invited to have a cup of refreshment, too.

Come to the beautiful Fox River Valley
and enjoy shopping for

Antiques in Batavia!

Village Antiques

Six dealers offering furniture, glassware,
collectibles and reproduction brass hardware

416 East Wilson Street • 630/406-0905
Tuesday-Saturday, 10-5; Sunday, 12-5

———

Pedals, Pumpers & Rolls

Player Pianos, Reproducers,
Nickelodeons, Restorations/Sales

240 East State Street • 630/879-5555
Tues.-Sat., 10-5; or by special appointment

———

Savery Shops

1885 Home Featuring American Primitives,
Accessories, Quality New Folk Art

14 N. Washington Ave. (Rt. 25) • 630/879-6825
Monday-Saturday, 10-5; Sunday, 12-5

———

Kenyon & Company

Located at Jacob's Junction (1843 Home)
Wilson Street at Washington Ave. (Rt. 25)

215 E. Wilson St. • 630/406-0665
Monday-Saturday, 10-5; Sunday 12-5

———

Yesterdays

10 dealers specializing in restored oak &
walnut furniture, jewelry, glassware & pottery

115 S. Batavia Ave. (Rt. 31) • 630/406-0524
Tuesday-Saturday, 10-5; Sunday, 12-5

Batavia

Kenyon & Company Antiques
215 E. Wilson St. (at Washington-Rt. 25)
Phone (630) 406-0665
Monday thru Saturday 10 to 5, Sunday 12 to 5.
Antiques, gifts, art, collectibles in the 1843 home.

The Savery Shops - 1885 Home
14 N. Washington Ave. (Rt. 25)
Phone (630) 879-6825
Monday thru Saturday 10 to 5, Sunday 12 to 5.
Primitives, early pine, antiques and collectibles.
Artesians offer folk art.

Pedals, Pumpers & Rolls, Ltd.
240 E. State St.
Phone (630) 879-5555
Tuesday thru Saturday 10 to 5, or by
special appointment.
Player pianos, old and new rolls, organs,
nickelodeons.

Village Antiques
416 E. Wilson
Phone (630) 406-0905
Tuesday thru Saturday 10 to 5, Sunday 12 to 5.
6 dealers bring you furniture, primitives, collectibles.

Yesterdays
115 S. Batavia Ave. (Rt. 31)
Phone (630) 406-0524
Tuesday thru Saturday 10 to 5, Sun. 12 to 5.
10 dealers specializing in restored oak and walnut
furniture, jewelry, glassware and pottery.

Maple Park

Josie's Country Shop Antiques
On Rt. 38, 5 miles east of DeKalb,
9 miles west of Rt. 47.
Phone 815/756-1920
Everyday 12 to 5.
4 barns full, 30 consignors.

Sycamore

Storeybook Antiques & Books
1325 E. State St. (Hwy. 64)
Phone 815/895-5910
Afternoons or by chance.
Books, Victoriana.

Need another copy?

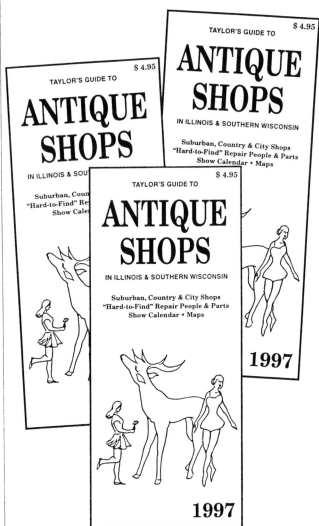

Sycamore *(continued)*

Bygone Era, Inc.
249 W. State St. (Rt. 64)
Phone 815/895-6538
7 days: 9 to 5:30, Mon. Thurs. Fri. 'til 9, Sun. 1 to 5.
On three levels, marbles to suites of furniture. Toys,
Nippon, wicker, sterling, primitives.

Continuing west on Rt. 64, see page 143.

DeKalb

Cracker Jax
118 N. Third St.
Phone 815/758-8178
Mon. thru Sat. 10 to 6, Sun. 12 to 5.
June to Aug. 15th: Mon. thru Sat. 12 to 6.
Antique (and later) jewelry, vintage clothing.

Kishwaukee Antiques
16075 S. First St. (corner of Elva Rd.)
Phone 815/756-9909
Tuesday thru Saturday 10 to 5, most of the time.
Victorian and country pieces, collectibles,
glassware, linens.

Kathleens Cupboard
323 E. Locust St.
Phone 815/758-2111
Tuesday Thru Saturday 10 to 3.
Many new decorative accessories and fine
collections in the old greyhound bus station.
Everything is for sale—display cupboards,
dry sinks, etc.

Friends & Company
203 E. Locust St.
Phone 815/758-3310
Tuesday thru Friday 10 to 5:30, Sat. 10 to 3.
Oak furniture, old farm toys, crafts, gourmet foods.

Esmond

Ashelford Hall
556 Eychaner Rd.
Phone 815/393-4845
By chance or appt.
Antique furniture, kitchen collectibles,
art deco items, Hot Wheels, Matchbox.

ANTIQUE MALLS

NAPERVILLE
Antique Mall
242 S. Washington
Naperville, IL
(630) 717-5511 & 717-9911

WHEATON
Antique Mall
1621 N. Main
Wheaton, IL
(630) 653-7400

PLANO/RT. 34
Antique Mall
420 W. Rt. 34
Plano, IL
*4-1/2 miles east of
Sandwich IL*
(630) 552-4478

RT. 59 Antique Mall
3S450 Rt. 59
Warrenville, IL
(9/10 mile N. of I-88)
(630) 393-0100
50 dealers • Outdoor Flea
Market • Auctions Bimonthly

NEW!

Chicagoland's Largest and Finest
Visit our 4 antique malls just minutes apart for hours of fun,
entertainment and money saving value. Over 200 of Chicago's
finest antique and collectible dealers, with plenty of parking, great
restaurants nearby, and helpful, friendly, knowledgeable sales people.

We also do:
Appraisals • Estate and House Sales • Consignments

HOURS: NAPERVILLE, WHEATON & WARRENVILLE:
Monday thru Saturday 10 to 5, Thurs. 'til 8, Sunday 12 to 4.
PLANO: Monday thru Saturday 10 to 5, Sunday 12 to 5,
Note: hours extended during Sandwich, Kane & DuPage Antique Shows

Area 8
WEST ON ROUTE 34

In this section: Hinsdale, Clarendon Hills, Westmont, Downers Grove, Lisle, Warrenville, Naperville, Plainfield, Oswego, Yorkville, Plano, Sandwich, Somonauk, Waterman

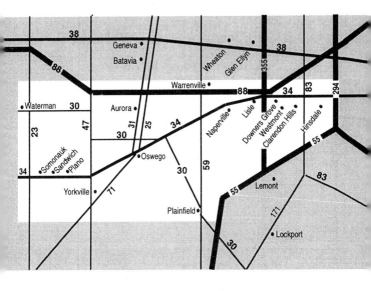

Hinsdale

Aloha's Antiques
6 W. Hinsdale Ave.
Phone (630) 325-3733
Tuesday thru Saturday 10 to 5.
Fine jewelry and keepsakes.

The Yankee Peddler
6 E. Hinsdale Ave.
Phone (630) 325-0085
Monday thru Saturday 10 to 5.
Antiques and specialty shop.

Robin's Egg Blue
30 E. Hinsdale Ave.
Phone (630) 325-1776
Monday thru Friday 10 to 5:30, Sat. 'til 5.
European pine, glassware, silver and reproduction furniture.

Griffin's in the Village
16 E. First St.
Phone (630) 323-4545
Monday thru Saturday 10 to 5.
Antiques among the silk flowers and home accessories.

Hinsdale *(continued)*

The Courtyard
63 Village Place
Phone (630) 323-1135
Tuesday thru Saturday 10 to 4:30.
*A consignment/donation shop that has furniture
and accessories, some are antique—check it out.*

Fleming & Simpson Ltd.
53 S. Washington, corner of First St.
Phone (630) 654-1890
Tuesday thru Saturday 10 to 5.
English furniture and silver, antique jewelry.

David Alan Antiques & Art
52 S. Washington - upstairs
Phone (630) 325-6090
Tuesday thru Saturday 11 to 5.
*Vintage & folk art, primitive cabinets, tables,
early 19th C. furniture & collectibles.*

Barbara Curtis Antiques
5900 S. Grant St.
Phone (630) 323-7914
Tues. thru Sat. 11 to 4. In Feb: Sat. only.
American, English country furniture, accessories.

Clarendon Hills

Ebeneezer Gift House
14 S. Prospect Ave.
Phone (630) 654-8882
Monday thru Saturday 10 to 5.
*Antique accent pieces, antique furniture,
more china and glassware upstairs.*

Westmont

Antiques on Old Plank Rd.
233 W. Ogden Ave. (at Park)
Phone (630) 971-0500
Tuesday thru Saturday 10 to 5, Sun. 12 to 5.
*Lots of furniture including English and Irish pine.
A large selection of decorative accessories. Also
garden urns & statues and wicker furniture.*

Tony's Antiques & Collectibles
141 S. Cass Ave.
Phone (630) 515-8510
Open occassionally.

Downers Grove

Asbury's Quality Antiques
1624-26 Ogden Ave.
Phone (630) 769-9191
Mon. thru Fri. 10 to 6, Thurs. 'til 8, Sat. 10 to 5.
*Fine furniture, glass, porcelain, oriental. A
separate room of repro antique furniture . Bronzes.*

Downers Grove *(continued)*

Treasures on Main Street
4912 Main St. (above Nancy's Tea Room)
Phone (630) 964-5515
Monday thru Saturday 11 to 3.
Shop upstairs for collectibles, depression
glass, jewelry & dolls. Have lunch in the Tea Room
downstairs. (They take lunch orders 'til 2 pm.)

About Time Antiques & Collectibles and Neat Stuff
932 Warren Ave. (in the Tivoli Theatre Building
1 block east of Main, north of RR track)
Phone (630) 968-7353
Mon. Wed. Fri. Sat. 11 to 5, Thurs. 'til 7,
closed Sunday and Tuesday.
Jewelry, toys and neat stuff.

Lisle

Antique Bazaar
924 Ogden Ave. (2 blocks east of Rt. 53)
Phone (630) 963-8282
Mon. thru Sat. 10 to 5, Thurs. 'til 8, Sun. 12 to 4.
Give yourself time to browse thru two floors
of antique architectural items, antiques and
collectibles. They also offer restoration services.

Lisle *(continued)*

Home Arcade Corp. of Lisle
1108 Front St. (just south of the viaduct)
Phone (630) 964-2555
Monday thru Saturday 9 to 5.
Jukeboxes, pinball & video games, antique slot
& peanut machines, old & new advertising.

Maison Russe
1720 Ogden Ave.
Phone (630) 963-5160
Monday thru Saturday 10 to 5, Sun. 1 to 4.
Russian collectibles, folk art, icons, samovars.
A touch of eastern Europe in the western suburbs.

Warrenville

Rt. 59 Antique Mall
3S450 Rt. 59 (approx. 1 mile N. of I-88)
Phone (630) 393-0100
Mon. thru Sat. 10 to 5, Thurs. 'til 8, Sun. 12 to 4.
50 dealers. Auctions held bimonthly.
Outdoor flea market.

Lil' Red Schoolhouse Antiques & Collectibles
3S463 Batavia Rd. (between Butterfield Rd.
and Warrenville Rd.)
Phone (630) 393-1040
Monday thru Saturday 10 to 5, Sun. 11 to 5.
The 1836 pine board floors and hand-hewed
beams are still rendering service. 13 dealers.

Elizabeth J. Antiques at Butterfield Garden Center
29W036 Butterfield Rd.
Phone (630) 393-1062
Monday thru Saturday 10 to 5, Sun. 10 to 4.
An absolutely charming shop in an unlikely location,
inside a garden center. While you're there, pick out
some azaleas to take home. Watch closely,—don't
pass it by.

Naperville

Gabriel's Trumpet
1163 E. Ogden Ave. in the Iroquois Center.
Phone (630) 420-2200
Mon. thru Sat. 10 to 5, Thurs. Fri. 'til 8, Sun. 12 to 4.
*A consignment shop with fine furniture, mirrors,
decorative accessories, jewelry, china and crystal.*

Mary's Antique Mall
34 W. Jefferson
Phone (630) 717-8899
Monday thru Saturday 10 to 5, Sun. 12 to 4.
*A large 2-floor mall in the heart of downtown
Naperville with 55 dealers.*

Nana's Cottage
122 S. Webster, Suite 101 (2 blocks west
of Washington, off Jefferson)
Phone (630) 357-5105
Tues. Wed. Thurs. 10 to 4, Fri. & Sat. 10 to 5,
Sunday 12 to 4.
*They offer early pressed glass, art glass,
furniture, vintage textiles, steins, marbles.*

Naperville Antique Mall
242 S. Washington St.
Phone (630) 717-5511 & 717-9911
Mon. thru Sat. 10 to 5, Thurs. 'til 8, Sun. 12 to 4.
*Also visit their 3 other malls in Wheaton,
Plano and Warrenville.*

Riverwalk Lighting & Gifts
401 S. Main St.
Phone (630) 357-0200
Mon. thru Fri. 9:30 to 5:30, Thurs. 'til 8, Sat. 9 to 5.
Antique and new lighting, lamp shades, lamp parts.

Plainfield

Plainfield Antique Mart
502 W. Lockport St.
Phone 815/436-1778
Monday thru Saturday 10 to 6, Sun. 11 to 5.

Plainfield (*continued*)

On the Sunnyside of the Street Antiques
515 W. Lockport St.
Phone 815/436-1342
Tuesday thru Saturday 10 to 5, Sun. 11 to 5.
Antique china and crystal. 5 dealers.

Victorian Rose Antique Shop
23364 Lincoln Hwy. (Rt. 30)
Phone 815/436-5334
Monday thru Saturday 10 to 5, Sun. 11 to 5.
Furniture, porcelain, smalls.

R & S. Antiques
23364 Lincoln Hwy. (Rt. 30)
7 days, 10 to 5.
Furniture, glassware, clocks.

Oswego

Oswego Antiques Market
Rt. 34 & Main St.
Phone (630) 554-3131
Monday thru Saturday 10 to 5, Sun. 11 to 5.
Large multi-dealer shop has something for everyone's collection.

Oswego *(continued)*

Bob's Antique Toys & Collectibles
23 Jefferson St. at Main
Phone (630) 554-3234
Tuesday thru Saturday 10 to 4, Sun. 12 to 4.
Toys, Lionel trains, miniatures, baseball cards, marbles.

Mary's Christmas Shop
(inside Bob's Antique Toys)
Year 'round Christmas memories of the 1940's and 1950's, specializing in ornaments.

Pennington, Ltd.
25 Jefferson St. at Main
Phone (630) 554-3311
Monday thru Saturday 10 to 5, Sun. 12 to 4.
Fine antique and estate jewelry. Antiques, curios, collectibles, Masonic items. Vita writes an interesting newletter about jewelry.

Yorkville

Yorkville Antique Center
708 S. Bridge St. (Rt. 47)
Phone (630) 553-0418
7 days 10 to 5.
A fine antique shop in this small town.

Hays & Co. Antiques
203 S. Bridge St. (Rt. 47)
Phone (630) 553-1044
Tuesday thru Saturday 9:30 to 4:30, Sun. 12 to 4:30.
Furniture, glassware.

Plano

Plano/Rt. 34 Antique Mall
420 W. Rt. 34 (4-1/2 miles east of Sandwich)
Phone (630) 552-4478
Monday thru Saturday 10 to 5, Sun. 12 to 5.
A rambling mall with many dealers.

Sandwich

Sandwich Antique Mart
2300 E. Route 34 (in the Village East Plaza,
east of town.)
Phone 815/786-6122
Monday thru Saturday 10 to 5, Sun. 11 to 5.
Collectibles, dolls, toys, furniture, jewelry.

Talk of the Town Antiques
2300 E. Route 34, (also in the Village East
Plaza, east of town.)
Phone 815/786-2730
Monday thru Saturday 10 to 5, Sun. 11 to 5.
Art glass, Victorian country furniture, clocks.

Mary's Old House of Antiques
128 S. Main St.
Phone 815/786-9609
7 days, 10 to 7.
*Old medical instruments, photographic &
scientific items and a general line.*

Sandwich *(continued)*

Sandwich Antiques Mall at the Brown Barn
108 N. Main St.
Phone 815/786-7000
Monday thru Saturday 10 to 5, Sun. 12 to 5.
The barn is carpeted and panelled and filled with 40 antique dealers.

C. J.'s Antiques & Collectibles
2 E. Railroad • Phone 815/786-6021
Wednesday thru Saturday 10 to 5, Sun. 12 to 5.

Antique Treasures
32 E. Railroad
Phone 815/786-8022
Tuesday thru Saturday 11 to 5, Sun. 12 to 5.

Grace Carolyn Dahlberg Antiques
1110 N. Latham St.
Phone 815/786-1890
"At Home" every Wednesday - call ahead.
Luncheon served while we talk "antique."

SHOW: Sandwich Antiques Market
The Fairgrounds - Rt. 34, 8 am to 4 pm. May 18,
June 22, July 27, Aug. 17, Sept. 28, Oct. 26, 1997.

Somonauk

House of 7 Fables - Antiques
300 E. Dale St. (1/2 block n. of Rt. 34 at the
corner of Sycamore St.) Phone 815/498-2289
7 days 9 to 5, advisable to call.
Mr. Shaw has been offering American furniture and accessories here for 36 years.

Country Corner Antiques
100 S. Depot St.•Phone 815/498-1105
Mon. thru Fri. 9 to 4, closed Wed. Thurs. 'til 7,
Saturday & Sunday 11 to 5.
Furniture, glassware, toys, jewelry, primitives.

Harmon's Attic
115 W. Rt. 34 •Phone 815/498-9533
Mon. thru Sat. 10 to 4, closed Wed., Sun. 10 to 3.
Glassware, collectibles, reproduction oak furniture.

Waterman

Whistlestop Antique Shoppe
248 W. Lincoln Hwy.
Phone 815/264-9003
Open 6 days 10 to 5, closed Tuesday.
Over 20 dealers on two levels.

Country Mill Square - Looking Back Antiques
140 W. Lincoln Hwy.
Phone 815/264-7771
Open 6 days 10 to 5, closed Tuesday.

Area 9
OAK PARK & SUBURBS

In this section: Oak Park, Forest Park, Berwyn, Riverside, LaGrange Park, LaGrange, LaGrange-Countryside, LaGrange Highlands, Lyons, Willow Springs.

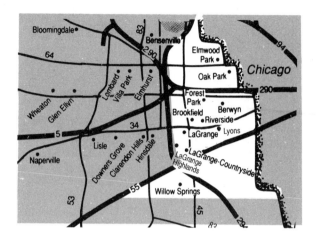

Oak Park

Antiques, etc. Mall
125 N. Marion
Phone (708) 386-9194
Mon. thru Fri. 11 to 7, Mon. & Thurs. 'til 8,
Sat. 11 to 5, Sun. 12 to 5.
Large mall in the heart of Oak Park.

> **The Jewelry, Studio/The Gold Hatpin**
> Located inside Antiques, etc. Mall
> *All periods of jewelry, including a case*
> *of Bakelite.*

John Toomey Gallery
818 North Blvd.
Phone (708) 383-5234
Open for preview one week before auction—
Saturday to Saturday 10 to 5, other times
by appointment.
Auctions of arts & crafts era and modern
pieces several times a year.

Kellar & Kellar Fine Arts & Antique Gallery
105 S. Ridgeland Ave.
Phone (708) 848-2882
Open by chance or appointment.
Oil paintings, works on paper, 19th and early
20th C. decorative art. Specializing in Japanese art.

Oak Park *(continued)*

Treasures & Trinkets
600 Harrison & East Ave.
Phone (708) 848-9142
Monday thru Friday 10 to 3, Sat. 10 to 4.
Costume jewelry, glassware, collectibles.

Forest Park

Antik Headd
7416 W. Madison St.
Phone (708) 366-7166
Tues. thru Fri. 10 to 6, Thurs 'til 8, Sat. 11 to 5.
Furniture & select vintage clothing.

Curiousities, Giftware & Collectibles
7439 W. Madison St.
Phone (708) 366-2030
Tuesday thru Saturday 10 to 6.
Knicknacks, pocket size collectibles, etc.

Atlantic Crossing
7501 W. Madison St.
Phone (708) 771-8400
Monday thru Friday 1 to 5, Sat. 10 to 4.
In the office of the moving & storage company.
Interesting
items from estates and abandoned storage.

Forest Park Antiques
7504 W. Madison St.
Phone (708) 366-0232
Open everyday 10 am, except Tues. by chance. Open
late Mondays and sometimes weekends.
*Furniture, glassware, sewing tools, railroad
memorabilia.*

At Home With Antiques
7516 W. Madison St.
Phone (708) 771-0608
Open 7 days: Mon. thru Fri. 11 to 6, Sat. 10 to 5,
Sunday 12 to 5.
*Eight dealers with everything from furniture to
smalls.*

Berwyn

Josie's Antiques & Collectibles
2135 S. Wisconsin (2 blocks east of Harlem Ave.,
just north of Cermak Rd.) • Phone (708) 788-3820.
Open a lot but no set hours. Take a chance or call.
*In a sturdy Berwyn brick bungalow with a store
front.*

Past Time Antiques
7100 W. 16th St. (corner of Wisconsin)
Phone (708) 788-4804
Thursday, Friday, Saturday 12 to 5.
A variety including wooden toy boats.

Berwyn *(continued)*

A & A Antiques
1609 S. Oak Park Ave.
Phone (708) 749-1970
Tuesday thru Sunday 10 to 3.
Furniture, glassware, lamps, etc.

Antique Treasure Chest
6746 W. 16th St.
Phone (708) 749-1910
Mon. Tues. Wed. 10 to 3, Thurs. Fri. Sat. 10 to 4.
Lots of furniture, stemware, dishes.

The Silver Swan
6738 W. 16th St.
Phone (708) 484-7177
Tuesday thru Saturday 10 to 2.
Silver, toys, china, glass, beer steins.

BBMM Antiques & Collectibles
6710 W. Cermak Rd.
Phone (708) 749-1465
Monday thru Saturday 10 to 6.
Dining room sets, chairs, Victorian furniture, glassware, lamps, etc.

The Player Piano Clinic
6810 W. 26th St.
Phone (708) 484-1020
Daily 10 to 5, closed Wed. & Sun. Thurs. 'til 8.
Closed Saturdays from June 1st to Sept. 1st. or by appt.
Always best to call ahead.
Player pianos, new and old piano rolls.

Rusnak's Antiques
6338 W. 26th St.
Phone (708) 788-4086
Usually open but best to call ahead.
China, furniture, glass, metals.

Riverside

Arcade Antiques & Jewelers
25 Forest Ave. (corner of East Ave.)
Phone (708) 442-8110
Tuesday thru Saturday 11 to 5, Sun. 12 to 4.
Grace and elegance best describe the jewelry and general line of antiques found here. Kay's shop will be number one on your top ten list.

Riverside Antique Market
30 East Ave.
Phone (708) 447-4425
Monday thru Saturday 11 to 5, Sun. 12 to 4.
12 rooms, nooks and crannies filled by 20 dealers

Riverside *(continued)*

J.P. Antiques
36 East Avenue
Phone (708) 442-6363
Tuesday thru Saturday 11 to 5, Sun. 12 to 4.
*Six rooms filled with an interesting collection
of antiques.*

Arcade Antiques & Furniture
7 Longcommon Rd. (Just across the parkway from
Arcade Antique & Jewelers. On the other side of the
historical watertower.)
Phone (708) 442-8999
Tuesday thru Saturday 11 to 5, Sun. 12 to 4.
*Kay's second shop featuring fine furniture, rugs,
pictures, lamps & beautiful accessories.*

LaGrange Park

LaGrange Park Antique Mall
1005 E. 31st St.
Phone (708) 482-3966
Mon. thru Sat. 11 to 6, Thurs. 'til 8, Sun. 11 to 5.
21 dealers.

LaGrange Park *(continued)*

31st Street Antiques
1017 E. 31st St. (1-1/2 miles east of Mannheim Rd.)
Phone (708) 352-1172
Mon. thru Fri. 11 to 6, Thurs. 'til 8,
Sat. 10 to 6, Sun. 11 to 5.
Furniture, jewelry, toys & marbles, advertising, etc.

Almost Anything Antiques
19 E. 31st (1 block east of Rt. 45)
Phone (708) 352-2232
Tues. thru Fri. 12 to 5, Sat. 11 to 5.
Everything is on consignment.

LaGrange

Antiques & More
2 S. Stone Ave. (7 blocks west of
Rt. 45, just south of the tracks)
Phone (708) 352-2214
Tuesday thru Saturday 10 to 5.
An interesting and varied collection.

Rosebud
729 Hillgrove-corner of Brainard, west of Rt.
45, north side of tracks.
Phone (708) 352-7673
Open 6 days: weekdays 11 to 5:30, closed Wed.
Sunday 12 to 4.
Furniture.

LaGrange-Countryside

LaGrange Antique Mall
35 E. Plainfield Rd. (just east of Rt. 45)
Phone (708) 352-9687
7 days 10 to 5, Mon. & Thurs. 'til 9.
*A large shop with a wide variety of antiques-
large and small.*

LaGrange Highlands

Antique & Vintage Traders
1510 W. 55th St. (1/2 mile east of Wolf Rd.)
Phone (708) 246-2415 or 246-3077
Monday thru Saturday 10 to 5, Thurs. 'til 7.
*A choice selection of antiques & vintage furniture
and accompanyments.*

Lyons

A Touch of Beauty, Brass & Lighting
7703 W. Joliet Rd. (43rd St.)
Phone (708) 442-5535
Saturday 10 to 3, or call for an appointment.
*Antique lighting and hardware for the home. Also
wind-up phonographs. Repair services, metal
smithing.*

Willow Springs

Glassware Matching Service
P.O. Box 207, Willow Springs, IL 60480
Call for appt: (708) 839-5231
*Matching service for depression, glass, Cambridge,
Heisey, Fostoria, etc.*

HISTORIC LEMONT
Restaurants • Antique Shops • Specialty Shops

*Start your exploration with
one of these fine merchants*

Antique Parlour • 316-318 Canal St. 630-257-0033.
Wed-Sun. 11-5. Fine furniture specializing in Mahogany &
Walnut, linens, lace; needlepoint, jewelry, silver, art and
Homethings -1840-1940, Gargoyle Studio angels, giftwraps.

Bittersweet Antiques & Country Accents
111 Stephen St. 630-243-1633. Open 7 days 10-4. Country
primitives, painted furniture, decoys, fishing lures and
woodenware. Country decorator items, lamps, candles, etc.

Carroll & Heffron Antiques & Collectibles
206 Stephen St. 630-257-0510. Mon-Fri 10-5, some weekends.
Some of our specialties include artwork, books, ceramics,
glassware, salt & peppers, furniture and toys.

Greta's Garret • 408 Main St. 630-257-0021. Tues-Sat 11-4.
Antiques, collectibles, art pottery, jewelry, Lenox china,
Carnival Glass, Dresden, glass shoes, glass animals.
Also Appraisals & Estate Sales.

Kenny's Advertising for the Ages • 206 Stephen St.
630-257-0510. Mon-Fri 10-5 some weekends. Antique &
collectible advertising: beer, whiskey, soda, tobacco and
pre-prohibition.

Lemont Antiques • 228 Main St. 630-257-1318. Daily 11-5
or appt. Clocks, watches, furniture, glass, dolls, cookie
jars, salt & peppers, primitives, Russian artifacts. Repairs:
timepieces, music boxes, phonographs, phones & lamps.

Me & My Sister • 206 Main St. 630-243-1769.
Me & My Sister invite you to visit our shop filled with
unique painted furniture, glassware, cards, candles
and many fine gifts.

Myles Antiques • 119 Stephen St. 630-243-1415.
Affordable elegance with a fine selection of European and
American furniture, quality home decorating accessories
and Fenton art glass.

Neena's Treasures For All Seasons • 44 Stephen St.
630-243-0533. Mon-Sat 10-5, Sun 12-4. Sample gourmet foods,
coffee and teas. Enjoy the beautiful treasures for your
decorating & gift giving needs. Christmas items all year.

A place with variety, spice & charm like no other
We think Lemont has what you are looking for.
All within 3 blocks • 30 minutes SW of Chicago
4 miles south of I-55 on Lemont Rd.

Area 10
SOUTHERN SUBURBS

Lemont, Lockport, Joliet, Morris, Homer Township, Orland Park, Frankfort, Oak Lawn, Evergreen Park, Chicago (111th & Western), Blue Island, Flossmoor, Steger, Crete, Beecher, Grant Park, Wilmington, Braidwood, Coal City, Bourbonnais, Kankakee, Manteno.

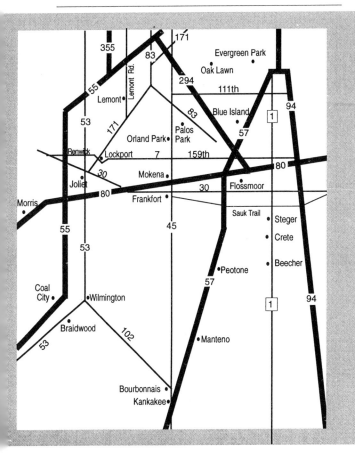

Lemont

Main St. Antique Emporium
220 Main St.
Phone (630) 257-3456
Mon. Tues. Wed. 11 to 5, Thurs. Fri. Sat. 'til 8,
Sunday 11 to 5.
2 floors of antiques.

Lemont Antiques
228 Main St.
Phone (630) 257-1318
7 days 11 to 5 or by appt.
Furniture, china, glass, clocks, watches, collectibles cookie jars and Russian artifacts.

Neena's **Treasures For All Seasons**

*Showcasing the Creations
of
53 Original Artisans
13 of which are exclusive*

Hand-Painted & Crafted Furniture
Including Children's
Custom Furniture & Mantels
Framed Original Works of Art
Collectible Bears
Hand-made Santas & Dolls
Lighthouses & Nauticals
Unique Birdhouses & Cages
Miniature Collectibles
French Copperware & Pewter
Gourmet Foods, Coffees & Teas

We Create Exquisite Customized Gifts

*Neena's Treasures
for
All Seasons
44 Stephen Street*

Historic Downtown Lemont
630-243-0533 * 8617 Fax

*Monday - Saturday 10 - 5
Sunday 12-4*

"Visit us soon, to experience beautiful Neena's !"
Allene
Proprietor

Lemont *(continued)*

Greta's Garret
408 Main St.
Phone (630) 257-0021
Tuesday thru Saturday 11 to 4.
*Originally a candy and school supply store,
built in 1850. Art pottery, jewelry, Lenox
china, etc.*

Antique Parlour
316-318 Canal St.
Phone (630) 257-0033
Wednesday thru Sunday 11 to 5.
*Antiques, furniture, linens, jewelry, in the
old (1928) Dodge dealer showroom.*

Myles Antiques
119 Stephen St.
Phone (630) 243-1415
7 days 10 to 4.
*Fine European & American furniture, accessories,
Fenton art glass fill this corner shop.*

Carroll & Heffron Antiques
206 Stephen St.
Phone (630) 257-0510
Monday thru Friday 10 to 5, some weekends.
*Artwork, books, toys, glass, ceramics
are some of the antiques you'll find here.*

Kenny's Advertising for the Ages
206 Stephen St.
Phone (630) 257-0510
Monday thru Friday 10 to 5, some weekends.
*Antique & collectible advertising of beer,
whiskey, soda, tobacco.*

Bittersweet Antiques & Country Accents
111 Stephen St.
Phone (630) 243-1633
Open 7 days 10 to 4.
*An 1885 limestone building filled with country
primitives, painted furniture, decoys, fishing lures.*

**The Strand Cafe, Ice Cream Parlor &
Antique Emporium**
103 Stephen St.
Phone (630) 257-2112
Open 7 days 8 am to 9 pm.
*A restaurant/antique shop where you can buy
the dishes - and everything else. Browse the 2nd floor.*

Neena's Treasures For All Seasons
44 Stephen St.
Phone (630) 243-0533
Monday thru Saturday 10 to 5, Sun. 12 to 4.
*A shop showing the work of 53 artisans - from
handmade Santas to handpainted furniture. The
wares blend beautifully with antiques.*

Lemont *(continued)*

Me & My Sister
206 Main St.
Phone (630) 243-1769
Tuesday thru Saturday 10 to 5, Sun. 12 to 4.
They paint and stencil old furniture and new glass-
ware. You'll also find candles, cards, gifts.

Lockport

Antiques on State
901 S. State St.
Phone 815/834-1974
Wednesday thru Saturday 11 to 5, Sun. 12 to 4.
The young owners have filled the shop with
interesting, fine antiques. Will the wax display lady,
with real hair and glass eyes, survive our hot
summers?

Canal House Antiques
905 S. State St.
Phone 815/838-8551
Wednesday thru Saturday 11 to 5, call ahead
advised.
Two floors of fine antiques carrying American 18th &
early 19th C. art, prints, fine furniture, silver, quilts,
etc. in a restored 1850's storefront building.

Ages Antiques, Collectibles, etc.
928 S. State St.
Phone 815/838-8540
Wednesday thru Friday open at 11, Sat. 11 to 5,
Sunday 12 to 5.
Metal toys, Fisher-Price, clocks.

Pastimes Cafe & Antiques
110 W. 10th St.
Phone 815/834-0993
Mon. thru Fri. 6 am to 3 pm, Sat. & Sun. 10 to 5.
A cafe/deli/bakery that also sells antiques.

Lockport *(continued)*

Lock's Antique Port
200 W. 11th St. (entrance is through the courtyard)
Phone 815/838-4570
7 days 10 to 5.
This mall is on the canal in an historic warehouse / brewery.
I loved the stenciled floors. Martha would be proud.

Joliet

Uniques Antiques Ltd.
1006 W. Jefferson St.
Phone 815/741-2466
Tuesday thru Saturday 11 to 5.
Furniture, hunting & fishing items, advertising.

Chicago Street Mercantile
178 North Chicago St.
Phone 815/722-8955
Tuesday thru Saturday 11 to 5.
Furniture & furnishings from 1800-1930.

Spies Antique Building Materials
228-230 E. Washington
Phone 815/722-5639
Open by chance or appt.
Architectural antiques: mantels, doors, backbars.

Morris

Morris Antique Emporium
112 W. Washington St.
Phone 815/941-0200
Mon. thru Fri. 10 to 7, Sat. 10 to 5, Sun. 12 to 5.
Located in an historic building, they have
3 floors of antiques.

Morris *(continued)*

Samantha Lynn's
117 W. Washington St.
Phone 815/941-0366
Monday thru Saturday 10 to 5.
Primitives and kitchen collectibles - also new gifts.

Repeat Boutique
124 E. Washington St.
Phone 815/941-0253
Monday thru Saturday 9 to 5.
Antiques and collectibles with resale clothing.

Allison's Cool Stuff
126 E. Washington St.
Phone 815/941-2175
Monday thru Saturday 9 to 5.
Nostalgic and fun stuff, jewelry.

Judith Ann's
117-119 W. Jackson
Phone 815/941-2717
Tuesday thru Saturday 10 to 5.
Glassware, furniture, Elvis collectibles, primitives.

Homer Township

Station House Antique Mall
12305 W. 159th St. (Rt. 7) East of
Lockport, 3 miles west of Orland Park.
Phone (708) 301-9400
7 days 10 to 6, Thurs. 'til 8.
Very nice antique mall with 50 dealers.

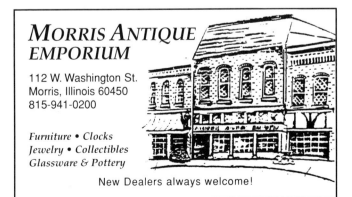

You're invited to visit . . .

Orland Park's

BEACON AVENUE ANTIQUE ROW

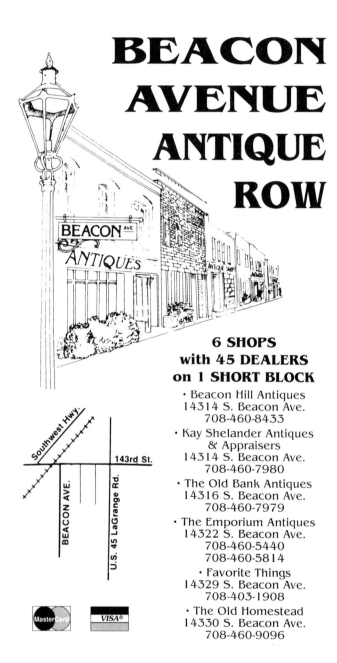

**6 SHOPS
with 45 DEALERS
on 1 SHORT BLOCK**

- Beacon Hill Antiques
  14314 S. Beacon Ave.
  708-460-8433
- Kay Shelander Antiques
  & Appraisers
  14314 S. Beacon Ave.
  708-460-7980
- The Old Bank Antiques
  14316 S. Beacon Ave.
  708-460-7979
- The Emporium Antiques
  14322 S. Beacon Ave.
  708-460-5440
  708-460-5814
- Favorite Things
  14329 S. Beacon Ave.
  708-403-1908
- The Old Homestead
  14330 S. Beacon Ave.
  708-460-9096

OPEN EVERYDAY
Monday thru Saturday 10:30 to 5 • Sunday 12:30 to 5

143rd St. & Beacon Ave. Orland Park, IL
(3 blocks west of Rt. 45)

230

Orland Park

Beacon Hill Antiques
14314 S. Beacon Ave.
Phone (708) 460-8433
Mon. thru Sat. 10:30 to 5, Sun. 12:30 to 5.
Furniture and a good mixture of antiques.

Kay Shelander Antiques & Appraisers
14314 S. Beacon Ave.
Phone (708) 460-7980
Mon. thru Sat. 10:30 to 5, Sun. 12:30 to 5.
Furniture and antique reference books

The Old Bank Antiques
14316 S. Beacon Ave.
Phone (708) 460-7979
Mon. thru Sat. 10:30 to 5, Sun. 12:30 to 5.
*Jewelry, glass, collectibles in this large
multi-dealer shop.*

The Emporium Antiques
14322 S. Beacon Ave.
Phone (708) 460-5440 & (708) 460-5814
Mon. thru Sat. 10:30 to 5, Sun. 12:30 to 5.
*Fine antique and vintage jewelry, furniture and
glassware fill 2 floors well stocked with these
antiques and more.*

The Old Homestead
14330 S. Beacon Ave.
Phone (708) 460-9096
Mon. thru Sat. 10:30 to 5, Sun. 12:30 to 5.
*Victorian and country antique furniture and
antique reproduction furniture integrated among
crystal, fine collectibles, floral designs.*

Favorite Things
14329 S. Beacon Ave.
Phone (708) 403-1908
Mon. thru Sat. 10:30 to 5, Sun. 12:30 to 5.
*Newest member of the "row" with a general line
that includes furniture, primitives and a room of
"pretties" for the ladies.*

The General Store
14314 Union Ave.
Phone (708) 349-9802
Mon. thru Sat. 10:30 to 5, Sun. 12:30 to 5.
16 dealers.

Cracker Barrel Antiques
9925 W. 143rd Place
Phone (708) 403-2221
7 days 11 to 5.
*Nice shop with a lot of pine & oak furniture. Mantels
and armoires. Also linens and baskets.*

232

Frankfort

The Trolley Barn
11 S. White St.
Phone 815/464-1120
Mon. thru Fri. 10 to 8, Sat. 10 to 6, Sun. 12 to 6.
43 dealers and 13 specialty shops (including 3 eating establishments and an ice cream shop) are housed in a renovated Trolley Barn.

Antiques Unique
100 Kansas St.
Phone 815/469-2741
Tuesday thru Saturday 10 to 5, Sun. 12 to 5.
There is always a handsome selection of Victorian jewelry, sterling , stained glass and more in Shirley's shop in "old Frankfort."

The Maggi Studio / Museum
119 W. Nebraska, in the historic district.
Phone ahead: 815/469-2424 for shop or museum tour.
Antique and collectible dolls, accessories.

Oak Lawn

Browsatorium, Inc.
9505 S. Cook Ave.
Phone (708) 423-8955
Monday thru Saturday 10 to 5, Sun. 11:30 to 4.
Lives up to its name - a fine shop filling two floors. Hilda is the charming owner. Located in a former stable built in 1910 for the Krueger Butcher Shop.
Furniture Refinishing Workshop
Phone (708) 423-0287

Shirley's Antiques
9650 S. Pulaski
Phone (708) 499-2300
Tuesday thru Saturday 10 to 5.
Furniture and general line.

Antique Safaris

Join your antique guides, intrepid explorers Grace Carolyn Dahlberg and Irene Taylor on day (sometimes 2-day) safaris to "Antique Country." Luxury buses and delicious lunches included in these fascinating forays to various antiques shops, malls and entire towns! Now in their 13th year, Antique Safaris have been led to various sites: urban, suburban and 'way out yonder. Trips are usually the first Saturday in May and October and leave from the Villa Park Historical Museum.

For information about custom trips for your club or group, call Irene 847-392-8438 or Grace Carolyn 815-786-1890.

To receive information about upcoming trips, send your name, address and phone number to:

Antique Safaris

202 N. Brighton Pl., Arlington Hts., IL 60004

Evergreen Park / Chicago

Aunt-Tiquery's
3300 W. 95th St.
Phone (708) 422-0677
Monday thru Saturday 10 to 5, Sun. 12 to 5.
Costume jewelry, china. Specializing in furniture.

The Crossings Antique Mall
1805 W. 95th St.
Phone (773) 881-3140
Monday thru Friday 10:30 to 6, Mon. & Thurs. 'til 7,
Sat. 10 to 5, Sun. 12 to 3.
20 dealers.

Chicago (Western Ave. & 111th St.)

Memories & More
10143 S. Western Ave.
Phone (773) 238-5645
Mon. thru Sat. 10 to 5, Sun. 12 to 5.
*Furniture a specialty, country, vintage clothing,
8 dealers.*

Cluttered Cupboard
10332 S. Western Ave.
Phone (773) 881-8803
Monday thru Saturday 10 to 5, Sun. 12 to 5.
Not as cluttered as some cupboards I've seen (mine)!

Grandma's Attic
1833 W. 103rd St.
Phone (773) 779-9726
Tuesday thru Saturday 10 to 5.
Antiques, fine furniture, collectibles, doll.

Grich Antiques
10857 S. Western Ave.
Phone (773) 233-8734
Monday thru Saturday 11 to 3.
Furniture, paintings, porcelains.

Time Was Antiques
10912 S. Western-Suite 4
Phone (773) 233-1750
Saturday 10 to 5:30, other days by appt.
Traditional furniture, antiques, collectibles.

Timeless Treasures
2412 W. 111th St.
Phone (773) 238-6073
Monday thru Saturday 11 to 4.
General line.

David McClain Antiques
2716 W. 111th St.
Phone (773) 239-4683
7 days 12 to 6.
Furniture, pottery, war memoribilia, etc.

HISTORIC
BLUE ❦ ISLAND

— EST. 1996 —

THREE SISTERS
A·N·T·I·Q·U·E M·A·L·L

OPEN EVERYDAY
Monday - Saturday – 10 AM to 6 PM ❦ Sunday – NOON to 5 PM

Featuring 75 of the Midwest's finest antique dealers.
In the heart of Blue Island's Historic District, this spacious
terra-cotta clad building features restored tin ceilings and
hardwood floors. Built in 1915 as the home of the
F. W. Woolworth Store, the United Cigar Company,
the Elks Club, and now the **Three Sisters Antique Mall**

DOUBLING IN SIZE IN 1997!

I-57 south to 127th Street – 1 mile west to Western Ave.
I-294 south to Cicero Ave/127th Street – 3 miles east
on 127th Street to Western Ave.
Just North of Ben Franklin Crafts ❦ MasterCard and Visa

708-597-3331

13042 S. WESTERN AVENUE
BLUE ISLAND ❦ ILLINOIS

Chicago (111th St.) *(continued)*

Chez Therese Antiques
3120 W. 111th St.
Phone (773) 881-0824
Monday thru Saturday 11 to 5.
From fine porcelain and glass to good furniture.

King Edwards Attic
3147 W. 111th St.
Phone (773) 429-0277
Tuesday thru Saturday 10 to 5.
From antiques to good used furniture.

Blue Island

Three Sisters Antique Mall
13042 S. Western Ave.
Phone (708) 597-3331
Monday thru Saturday 10 to 6, Sun. 12 to 5.
A new mall in the F. W. Woolworth building built in 1915. Has the original tin ceilings and terra cotta front.

Encores
13117 S. Western Ave.
Phone (708) 389-4121
Monday thru Saturday 10:30 to 5.
General line.

Flossmoor

Loon Lake Ltd.
2557 Flossmoor Rd.
Phone (708) 957-3636
Tuesday thru Saturday 1 to 5.
Furniture, porcelain, silver, folk art and paintings.

Steger

Now & Then Shops
3725-29 Chicago Rd. (Rt. 1)
Phone (708) 755-9591
Tuesday thru Saturday 10:30 to 4:30, Sun. 12 to 4.
You'll find a wide range of antiques here, from primitive to precious.

Crete

Crete Antiques
502 Fifth St.
Phone (708) 672-4188
Tuesday thru Saturday 11 to 4, Sun. 11 to 5.
General line.

The Market Place
550 Exchange St.
Phone (708) 672-5556
7 days, 10 to 5.
Crete's oldest and largest shop.

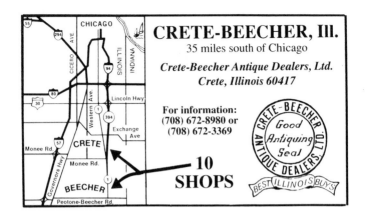

Crete *(continued)*

The Finishing Touch
563 Exchange St.
Phone (708) 672-9520
Monday thru Saturday 9 to 5.
Antiques, gifts and beautiful flowers.

Village Antiques & Lamp Shop
595 Exchange St.
Phone (708) 672-8980
Tuesday thru Saturday 10 to 5, Sun. 12 to 5.
General line, loads of lamps. Repair lamps.

The Farmer's Daughter
1246 Lincoln
Phone (708) 672-4588
Tuesday thru Saturday 10 to 5, Sun. 12 to 4.
The shop is in the barn of Fairview
Farm built in 1877.

Third Generation Antiques
1362 W. Exchange St.
Phone (708) 672-3369
Tuesday thru Saturday 10 to 5, Sun. 12 to 5.
Collectibles, toys, jewelry, furniture, etc.

Gatherings
1375 Main St.
Phone (708) 672-9880
Tuesday thru Saturday 10 to 5, Sun. 12 to 5.
Home accessories, architectural items, linens.

Seasons
1362 Main St.
Phone (708) 672-0170
Tuesday thru Saturday 10 to 5, Sun. 12 to 5.
Glassware, primitives, sports collectibles.

Crete *(continued)*

The Indian Wheel Company
1366 Main St.
Phone (708) 672-9612
Tues. thru Sat. 10 to 5, Sun. 12 to 5.
*Antiques, Southwest Indian artifacts,
collectibles, glassware.*

Antique Mall
509 Dixie Hwy.
Phone (708) 946-2264
By chance.

Beecher

Woodstill's Antiques
610 Gould St.
Phone (708) 946-3161
Wednesday thru Saturday 10 to 5, Sun. 12 to 5.
Furniture and a general line.

Homewood

The Treasure Trove
18148 Martin Ave.
Phone (708) 798-5522
Wednesday thru Saturday 10 to 4.

Grant Park

Sentimental Journey Antiques
111 S. Main St.
Phone 815/465-6100
Thursday thru Sunday 10 to 5.
*Antiques and collectibles including
depression glass and dolls.*

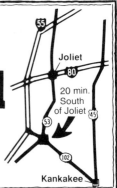

Wilmington

Most shops are within 2 blocks on
Water St. (north of the stoplight.)

Stuff & Such
111 N. Water St.
Phone 815/476-0411
Tuesday thru Saturday 10 to 5, Sun. 12 to 4.
Antiques, collectibles, crafts.

Abacus Antiques
113 N. Water St
Phone 815/476-5727
7 days, 10 to 5.
*Sports memoribilia, art deco &
nouveau lighting, pottery.*

Doves Cove
117 N. Water St.
Phone 815/476-1640
Open 7 days 10 to 5.
*A general line of antiques from the 1800's
thru the 1940s.*

Water Street Antique Mall
119-121 N. Water St.
Phone 815/476-5900
7 days, 10 to 5.
*Antiques on 3 levels. 24 dealers.
Antique furniture, collectibles, glassware.
40's-50's items, Fenton art glass.*

C & S Comics
215 N. Water St.
Phone 815/476-6616
Wed. thru Sun. 12 to 5.
New & collectible comics, baseball cards.

Paraphernalia Antiques
124 N. Water St. (Warehouse at the end of the
block.)
(see listing of Paraphernalia at 112 Water St.)

R. J. Relics
120 N. Water St. (enter thru Kaveney's)
Phone 815/476-6273
7 days, 10 to 5.
*Specializing in oak furniture, pocket knives,
old radios.*

Kaveney's Antiques
118 N. Water St.
Phone 815/476-5061
7 days, 10 to 5.
Two floors of antiques, collectibles, jewelry.

Wilmington *(continued)*

Paraphernalia Antiques
112 & 114 N. Water St.
Phone 815/476-9841
Mon. thru Fri. 9 to 5, Sat. 9 to 6, Sun. 11 to 6.
*Estate jewelry and Irish pine a specialty. Torquay.
Direct importer from the British isles and the
continent.*

Mill Race Emporium
110 N. Water St.
Phone 815/476-7660
Monday thru Saturday 10 to 5, Sun. 11 to 5.
*Antiques and collectibles on the main floor
and terrace level. 20 dealers.*

Mill Town Market
508 N. Kankakee St.
Phone 815/476-0386
Monday thru Saturday 10 to 5, Sun. 12 to 5.
*The newest mall in Wilmington with antiques,
old jewelry, crafts, giftware.*

Faulkners Emporium
605 E. Baltimore (Rt. 53) • Phone 815/476-2210
Mon thru Sat. 10 to 5, Sun. 11 to 5, Tues. & Thurs.
by chance. *Prints, paintings, serious primitives.
Owner knows a lot about genealogy.*

Braidwood

Ye-Olde-Cane Shoppe
151 N. Will Rd. (I-55 & Reed Rd. exit 233)
Phone 815/458-2090
Monday thru Saturday 8 to 2, Sun. by chance.
*Large warehouse, specializing in oak furniture.
Fred does caning and wicker repair.*

Coal City

Sheryl's Doll Clinic
135 S. Broadway
Phone 815/634-4605
Monday thru Friday 10 to 5, Sat. 10 to 2.
*Dolls, antique, new & collectible and doll
accessories. Dolls dressed and restored.*

Collector's Corner
355 S. Broadway
Phone 815/634-3345
Mon. thru Fri. 11 to 7 (not always open Fri.)
Military items: Civil war thru WWII.

Victoria's
660 Division St. (Rt. 113)
Phone 815/634-4563
Monday thru Saturday 10 to 4.
*Collectibles, oak furniture, carnival & depression
glass.*

Coal City *(continued)*

Then & Now Antiques & Collectibles
2090 Division St. (Rt. 113)
Phone 815/634-3527
Tuesday thru Friday 9:30 to 6, Sat. 9 to 4.
Variety including crafts.

Bourbonnais

Old Barn Antiques
1992 W. Rt. 102 (1-1/2 miles west of Latham Rd.)
Phone 815/939-4352 or 815/939-0052
Saturday & Sunday 10 to 4.
Large pieces of furniture, armoires, some smalls.

Indian Oaks Antique Mall
North Rt. 50 & Larry Power Rd.
(from I-57, exit Bradley 315, then go north)
Phone 815/933-9998
7 days, 10 to 5:30, Thurs. & Fri. 'til 8.
150 dealers.

Castle Antique Mall
1789 Rt. 50 N.
Phone 815/936-1505
7 days, 10 to 5.
120 dealers.

Kankakee

Kankakee Antique Mall
145 S. Schuyler Ave. (just off Rt. 17, east of Rt. 102)
Phone 815/937-4957
7 days 10 to 6.
Big, rambling building with 160 dealers.

Blue Dog Antiques
440 N. 5th Ave.
Phone 815/936-1701
Mon. thru Fri. 10 to 5, Sat. & Sun. by chance.
Multi-dealer mall.

Kankakee *(continued)*

Bell Flower Antiques
397 South Wall St. (Rt. 113)
Phone 815/935-8242
Evenings 5:30 to 8, Sat. & Sun. 10:30 to 5.

Manteno

Manteno Antique Mall
35 E. 3rd St.
Phone 815/468-0114
Open 7 days 10 to 5.
80 dealers.

Darters Antique Interiors
126 S. Locust (Rt. 50)
Phone 815/468-3675
Saturday & Sunday 12 to 5.
*In business for 26 years specializing
in Victorian furniture.*

Main Street Antiques
131 N. Main St.
Phone 815/468-6486
Saturday & Sunday 1 to 4.

Whether your antiquing takes you nationwide or statewide we can "TELL YOU WHERE TO GO" !!

"NO-NONSENSE"
ANTIQUE MALL DIRECTORY

The ultimate traveler's guide to more than 5,000 Antique Malls Antique Centers & Multi-Dealer shops in all 48 contiguous states

* Arranged alphabebtically by state/city for easy reference
* Standardized layout and format for all listed shops
* Includes all available information on shop size, hours & directions
* Provides cities' Rand-McNally Road Atlas map location
* Soft-cover, spiral bound 8.5" x 14" size fits in your Road Atlas

48 state, 5,000 + listings directory Price $20.50

price include 4th class postage; first class postage $1.75 extra
Still not sure??? For more information & free sample page, send SASE

To order before 6/1/97, send order and payment directory to:

FDS Antiques, Inc.
62 Blue Ridge Drive
Stamford, CT 06903-4923
Phone: 203-322-1753   FAX: 203-968-9564

Note: New Address After 6/1/97

P.O. Box 147, Higginsport, OH 45131

Now That You Know Where the Antique Shops are in Illinois. How About Manhattan? New Jersey? Pennsylvania? Ohio?

The Answer is in these two publications

Antique Shops of Manhattan
Over 800 entries
and

Antique Shops of NJ, PA & Ohio
Over 2000 entries
$9.95 each

To order send your check to Anacus Press P. O. Box 4544, Warren, NJ 07059. Add $2.00 to each order for shipping. New Jersey residents add 6% sales tax.

Looking for primitives, postcards or purses?
See
"Specialties in the Shops of the Advertisers"
starting on page 257.

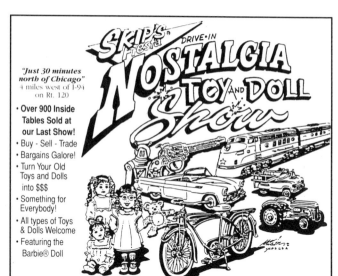

1997
Antique Shows
Mark your calendars!

April

11-12-13 .... Rosemont, Ill.
Convention Center, 5600 River Rd. *O'Hare Show.*

18-19 .... Countryside, Ill.
Engineer's Hall, 6200 Joliet Rd.
Greater Chicago Postcard Show.

18 thru 27 .... Chicago
Zigurat Architectural, 1702 N. Milwaukee Ave.
Stained glass show — past to present.

24-25-26-27 .... Bourbonnais, Ill.
Northfield Square Mall

25-26-27 .... Oak Park, Ill.
Chaney Mansion, 220 N. Euclid. *5th Annual.*

26-27 .... Palatine, Ill.
Harper College, Euclid, Algonquin & Roselle Rds.
Chicago Tribal Antique Show.

26-27 .... Princeton, Ill.
Bureau County Fairground. *19th Annual.*

27 .... St. Charles, Ill.
Kane County Fairground, Rt. 64 & Randall Rd.
Antique Toy & Doll World Show.

May

3-4 .... Highland Park, Ill.
Highland Park Community House, Sheridan & Elm Place.
Objects of style - best of 2 centuries.

18 .... Maquoketa, Iowa
Banowetz Antique Mall, Jct. Hwy 61 & 64.
Outdoor Antiques & Collector Fair.

25 .... Grayslake, Ill.
Lake County Fairground, Rt. 45 & Rt. 120.
Nostalgia Toy & Doll Show.

May 31-June 1 .... Glenview, Ill.
The Grove Center, 1421 Milwaukee Ave. *Antique Show.*

May 31-June 1 .... Riverside, Ill.
Downtown Riverside, Centennial Park & East Ave.
Spring Antique Faire.

May 31-June 1 .... Chicago
Dearborn St. between Congress & Polk Sts.
Printers Row Book Fair. Antique, rare & new books.

DUPAGE
Antique &
Collectible
Market

3rd Sunday of each month - 7 am to 4 pm
DuPage County Fairgrounds • Wheaton, Illinois
Between Rt. 38 & Rt. 64 on Manchester Rd. near County Farm Rd.

1997

April 20	Sept. 21
May 18	Oct. 19
June 15	Nov. 16
July - No show	Dec. 21
Aug. 17	**1998**
*Aug. 23/24	Jan. 18
	Feb. 15
*All Night Flea Market	March 15
	April 19

Hundreds of dealers • Indoors & Outside •
with beautiful, affordable antiques & collectibles.
*Furniture • Jewelry • Toys • Glassware • Art Pottery
Paper • Books • Primitives • and much more !*

FREE PARKING

Delicious home made food
Breakfast served. . .Lunch served all day.

FOR INFO: 847-455-6090

Admission $3.00

Sponsored by 4-H
of DuPage County

Marilyn Sugarman, manager

visit us at http://www.dupagefleamkt.pair.com

June

May 31-June 1 .... Glenview, Ill.
The Grove Center, 1421 Milwaukee Ave. *Antique Show.*

May 31-June 1 .... Riverside, Ill.
Downtown Riverside, Centennial Park & East Ave.
Spring Antique Faire.

May 31-June 1 .... Chicago
Dearborn St. between Congress & Polk Sts.
Printers Row Book Fair. Antique, rare & new books.

6-7-8 .... Lake Forest, Ill.
Lake Forest Academy, Rt. 60 (W. Kennedy Rd.)

7 .... St. Charles, Ill.
Leroy Oakes Forest Preserve, Dean St.
"A Day in the Country"

7-8 .... Chicago
Between Fullerton, Clark, Deming & Orchard St.
Park West Outdoor Antique Show. 34th annual.

20-21-22 .... Chicago
Navy Pier, Grand Ave & Lake Michigan

13-14-15 (opens at 5 pm June 13).......... Delafield, Wis.
Jefferson Building, 514 Wells St.
Lang's Delafield Antique Show.

14-15 .... Union, Ill.
Antique Village, 8512 So. Union Rd. (Marengo exit
off I-90.) *International Antique Music Sale.*

20-21-22 .... Niles, Ill.
Golf Mill Mall, Milwaukee Ave. & Golf Rd.

28 .... Barrington, Ill.
Northwest Hwy. (Rt. 14), between Lake-Cook Rd.
& Rt. 59. (The show is held in a large shaded area.)
Barrington Area Historical Society Tail Gate Show.

*Note: The dates on this calendar have
been confirmed but are subject to
change and other mishaps after we
have gone to press.*

July

2-3-4-5-6 .... Mt. Prospect, Ill.
Randhurst Shopping Center, Rt. 83 & Euclid Ave.

3-4-5-6 .... Maquoketa, Iowa
Banowetz Antique Mall, Jct. Hwy. 61 & 64.

5 .... Rosemont, Ill.
Holiday Inn O'Hare.
National Antique Lamp Show & Sale, 9am to 3 pm.

20 .... Naperville, Ill.
Naperville Holiday Inn. 1801 Naper Blvd.
Doll & Teddy Bear Show.

August

1-2 .... Countryside, Ill.
Engineer's Hall, 6200 Joliet Rd.
Greater Chicago Postcard Show.

8-9-10 .... Lake Geneva, Wis.
Church &Horticultural Hall, 320-330 Broad St.

10 .... Rosemont, Ill.
Sofitel Hotel, 5550 N. River R.
Barbie Goes to Chicago.

16 .... Maquoketa, Iowa
Banowetz Antique Mall, Jct. Hwy. 61 & 64
Antique & Custom Auto Show.

22-23-24 .... Rosemont, Ill.
Convention Center, 5600 River Rd. *O'Hare Show.*

25 .... St. Charles, Ill.
Kane County Fairgrounds, Randall Rd.
Doll & Bear Show & Sale.

30 .... Delafield, Wis.
Dept. of Public Works Building.
Benefit Hawks Inn Historical Society.

***See page 255 for Antique Sales/Flea Markets
at the Fairgrounds***

September

5-6 (Open 5 pm Sept. 5) .... Elgin, Ill.
Hemmens Auditorium. Grove Ave. at the Fox River.
Midwest Vintage Clothing & Jewelry Show.

5-6-7 .... Niles, Ill.
Golf Mill Mall, Milwaukee Ave. (Rt. 21) & Golf Rd.

6 .... Lake Forest, Ill.
Kennedy Rd. (Rt. 60), 1/2 mile west of Hwy. 41.
Infant Welfare Outdoor Tail-Gate Show.

6-7 .... Woodstock, Ill.
McHenry Cnty. Fairground, Country Club Rd. & Rt. 47.

12-13-14 .... Hinsdale, Ill.
Hinsdale Community House, 415 W. 8th St.

14 .... Maquoketa, Iowa
Banowetz Antique Mall, Jct. 61 & 64
Outdoor Antique & Collector's Fair.

13-14 .... Crete, Ill.
Balmoral Race Track, Route 1.

20 .... Cambridge, Wis.
Cambridge Village Square, Main St.
"A Day in the Park." Over 40 dealers.

21 .... St. Charles, Ill.
Kane County Fairgrounds. Randall Rd.
Doll & Bear Show - 3 buildings.

26-27-28 .... Waukesha, Wis.
Waukesha Expo Center - Forum Bldg.

28 .... Westmont, Ill.
Inland Meeting & Expo Center, 400 E. Ogden.
Doll & Teddy Bear Show, "Juneau to Ginny."

*Note: The dates on this calendar have
been confirmed but are subject to
change and other mishaps after we
have gone to press.*

October

2-3-4-5 .... Mt. Prospect, Ill.
Randhurst Shopping Center, Rt. 83 & Euclid.

3-4-5 .... Milwaukee, Wis.
Mackie Building, 225 E. Michigan St. Grain
Exchange room. *Milwaukee County Historical
Society. 14th annual.*

12 .... Bloomington, Ill.
Inter State Center, 2301 W. Market St. (Rt. 9)
Dolls, Toys, Bears, Miniatures.

16-17-18 .... Chicago.
Merchandise Mart, Wells St. at Chicago River.
Restoration / Chicago 97.

16-17-18-19 .... Kenosha, Wis.
Factory Outlet Centre, I-94 & Rt. 50.

18-19 .... St. Charles, Ill.
Kane County Fairground, Rt. 64 & Randall Rd.
Fox River Valley Antique Show.

23-24-25-26 .... Madison, Wis.
Westgate Mall.

24-25-26 .... Arlington Heights, Ill.
Arlington International Racecourse, Northwest
Hwy., Wilke & Euclid.

24-25-26 .... Chicago
Sacred Heart School, 6250 Sheridan Rd.

26 .... St. Charles, Ill.
Kane County Fairground, Rt. 64 & Randall Rd.
The Antique Toy & Doll World Show.

Oct. 31-Nov. 1 .... Countryside, Ill.
Engineer's Hall, 6200 Joliet Rd. - 1 block west of
LaGrange Rd. (Rt. 45).
Greater Chicago Postcard Show.

*See page 255 for Antique Sales/Flea Markets
at the Fairgrounds*

November

1-2 .... Cedarburg, Wis.
Cedarburg High School, W68N611 Evergreen Blvd.

6-7-8-9 .... Bourbonnais, Ill.
Northfield Square Mall.

7-8-9 .... Rosemont, Ill.
Convention Center, 5600 River Rd. *O'Hare Show.*

8-9 .... Winnetka, Ill.
Winnetka Community House, 620 Lincoln Ave.
Winnetka Modernism Show - 1890 to 1960.

14-15-16 .... St. Charles, Ill
Pheasant Run Mega Center, Rt. 64.

14-15-16 .... Naperville, Ill.
North Central College Fieldhouse.

16 .... St. Charles, Ill.
Kane County Fairgrounds, Randall Rd.
Holiday Doll & Bears & Toys Show & Sale .

22-23 .... Rockford, Ill.
Forest Hills Lodge, 990 Forest Hills Rd.
The 6th Annual Rock River Valley Antique Show.

1998

Jan. 16-17-18, 1998 .... Oakbrook, Ill.
Oakbrook Drury Lane (just north of shopping center)
Sponsored by the Fra Angelico Art Foundation.

Jan. 23-24-25, 1998 .... Palatine, Ill.
Harper College, Euclid, Algonquin & Roselle Rd.

Feb. 6-7-8 .... Waukesha, Wis.
Waukesha Expo Center, Forum Bldg.

March 13-14-15 .... St. Charles, Ill.
Pheasant Run Mega Center, Rt. 64.

May 12-3-4 .... Chicago
Merchandise Mart, Wells St. at Chicago River.
Chicago International Antique & Fine Art Fair.

Antique Sales
Flea Markets

at the Fairgrounds & Parks

ST. CHARLES, ILL. (1st Sunday of the month & preceding Saturday)
KANE COUNTY ANTIQUE FLEA MARKET, INC. at the Kane County Fairground, Randall Rd. (between Rt. 64 & Rt. 38), St. Charles, Ill. 1st Sunday and preceding Saturday of every month. Saturday 1 pm to 5 pm, Sunday 7 am to 4 pm. (See ad page 256.)

GRAYSLAKE, ILL. (2nd Sunday of the month)
ANTIQUES & COLLECTIBLES SHOW & SALE. Lake County Fairgrounds, Grayslake, Ill. Rt. 120 & U.S. 45. 2nd Sunday of every month, 8 am to 4 pm. (See ad page 250.)

WHEATON, ILL. (3rd Sunday of the month)
DUPAGE ANTIQUE AND COLLECTIBLE MARKET. DuPage County Fairground, Wheaton, Ill. Manchester Rd., between Rt. 38 & Rt. 64. 3rd Sunday of each month, 7 am to 4 pm. No show in July. (See ad page 248)

WHEATON, ILL. August 23-24, 1997
ALL NIGHT FLEA MARKET, DuPage County Fairgrounds, Manchester Rd.., between Rt. 38 & Rt. 64, near County Farm Rd. Opens 5 pm Saturday thru the night 'til 9 am Sunday. (See ad page 18.)

SANDWICH, ILL. (6 Sundays in 1997)
SANDWICH ANTIQUES MARKET. Sandwich Fairground, Rt. 34. SUNDAYS: May 18 June 22, July 27, Aug. 17, Sept. 28 Oct. 26. 8 am to 4 pm. (See ad page 10.)

UNION GROVE, WISCONSIN (3 Sundays in 1997)
RACINE ANTIQUES FAIR. Racine County Fairgrounds, Hwy. 11, 5 miles west of I-94. SUNDAYS: June 29, Aug. 3, Sept. 14. 8 am to 4 pm. (See ad page 159.)

PRINCETON, WISCONSIN (Every Saturday April 26-Oct. 18)
PRINCETON FLEA MARKET, Princeton City Park, Hwy. 23/73. Saturdays.(See ad page 23.)

SpecialtieS
in shops of our Advertisers

The catagories listed here notes antiques generally found in the shops listed—call to confirm.

SERVICES AND REPAIRS See Page 19

Door & Window Hardware
Al Bar 2
Baroque Silversmith 9
Bellows Shoppe 12
Donegan, Craig, Interior Artisan 69
Jan's Antiques 29
Renovation Source 55
Village Antiques 198
Embroideries, Oriental
Jade Butterfly Antiquities 117
English Accessories
Curiosity Shop 103
English Antiques
Antique & Vintage Traders 221
Cracker Barrel 232
Curiosity Shop 103
Heritage Trail Mall 70
Marsh Hill Ltd. 165
Ridgefield Merchants 124
English Silver
Silver Treasures 26
Ephemera
Eureka 68
Equine Specialties
Fourth Street Galleries 194
European Collectibles
Grandma's Attic 122
Fabrics, Provencal
Pied-A-Terre 79
Fiesta
Antiques Mart of Elk Grove 110
Fine Art
Antique & Porcelain by G.K. 84
Hebron Antique Gallery 133
Kellar & Kellar 214
Fishing Collectibles
Mary's Antique Mall 208
Firearms (antique)
Duffy's Attic 92
Fireplace Accessories
Bellows Shoppe 12
Town & Country 84
Fireplace, Victorian Tiles
A Touch of Beauty 216
Flatware, Silverplate
Petersen Silver Matching 73
Whippletree Farm 104
Flatware, Sterling
Set Your Table (matching) 73
Silver Treasures 26
M. Stefanich Antiques 78
Whippletree Farm 104
Floral Designs (Permanent)
Crystal Magnolia 96
Flow Blue
Antiques Unique 232
Antiques Center of Illinois 98
Bank Street Antiques 3
Maison Russe 206
Town & Country 84
Folk Art
Antiques Centre, The 32
Country Shop 80
FolkWorks Gallery 64
Hebron Antique Gallery 133
Harvey Antiques 66
Neena's Treasures 224
Savery Shops 198
Shops on Scranton 90
40's, 50's, 60's Memoribilia
1905 Emporium 129
Antique Emporium 118
Grafton Antique Mall 169
Home Arcade 207
Uniques Antiques 227
40's thru 70's Decorative Arts
Echoes Report 212
Three Sisters Antique Mall 236
Urban Artifacts 46

Fountain Pens
Mary's Antique Mall 208
Nana's Cottage 209
Rindfleisch Antiques 179
Fostoria Glass
Glassware Matching Service 194
Memory Lane 151
French Antiques
Antique & Vintage Traders 221
D & R International 148
Galleria 773 28
Pariscope 190
French Country Accessories
Pied-A-Terre 79
Furnishings, 20th C. Industrial design
Modernism Gallery of Chicago 4
ZigZag 49
Furniture
31st Street Antiques 220
A Matter of Time 114
A Step in the Past 194
Nancy Andrich 170
Anamosa Antiques 93
Antique Alley 174
Antique Bazaar 206
Antique Emporium 118
Antiques & Decorative Arts 120
Antiques & Porcelain by G.K. 84
Antiques Mart of Elk Grove 110
Antiques on Broadway 128
Arcade Antiques 219
Armitage Antique Gallery 44
At Home with Antiques 216
Banowetz Antiques 147
Beacon Avenue 230
Benson Corners 157
Cambridge Antique Mall 183
Carriage Antiques 123
Colonial Antiques 107
Cracker Barrel Antiques 232
Cupid's Antiques 186
Dairy Barn 132
Dickens of a Place 162
Direct Auction Gallery 58
Dove's Cove 240
Duffy's Attic 92
Evanstonia Period Furniture 66
FolkWorks Gallery 64
Fourth Street Galleries 194
Freddy Bear's Antique Mall 176
Gabriel's Trumpet 209
Gallery of Antiques 158
General Antique Store 181
Grandma's Attic 122
Heather Higgins Antiques 78
Heavenly Haven Antique Mall 177
Hebron Antique Gallery 133
Heritage Trail Mall 70
Interiors Anew 124
International Antiques Centre 46
Kane County Antique Flea Mkt. 256
LaGrange Antique Mall 221
Lake Geneva Antique Mall 173
Lost Eras 61
Memory Merchant 190
Midwestern Antiques & Art 61
Miracle on 58th Street 152
Morris Antique Emporium 229
Museum Country Store 110
Oakton St. Antique Center 108
Penny Lane Antiques 123
Pink Geranium 116
Port Antiques 171
Rebecca Anne Lincolnshire 100
Ridgefield Merchants 124
Rindfleisch Antiques 177
Shops on Scranton 90
Three Sisters Antique Mall 236
Uniques Antiques 227
Valenti Antiques 154

Specialties of the Advertisers *(continued)*

Glassware (cont.)
Gallery of Antiques 158
General Antique Store 181
Geneva Antique Market 194
Glassware Matching Service 194
Heavenly Haven Antique Mall 177
Interiors Anew 124
Lake Geneva Antique Mall 173
Lost Eras 61
Memory Lane 151
Midwestern Arts & Antiques 61
Miracle on 58th Street 152
Morris Antique Emporium 229
Penny Lane 123
Ridgefield Merchants 124
Sarah Bustle 62
Secret Treasures 68
Set Your Table (matching) 73
Shops on Scranton 90
Silk 'n Things 116

Stagecoach Antiques & Jewelry 188
Storm Hall Antique Mall 156
Three Sisters Antique Mall 236
Valenti Antiques 154
Glassware (new)
The Crystal Cave 261
Guides to Antique Shops 228
Gumball/Peanut Machines
Home Arcade 207
Hardware
A Touch of Beauty 216
Antique Bazaar 206
Bellows Shoppe 12
Donegan, Craig, Interior Artisan 67
Renovation Source 55
Haviland China Video 72
Heisey Glass
Glassware Matching Service 194
Water Street Antique Mall 240
Set Your Table 73

Multi-Dealer Shops

*Where you will find all categories
of antiques & collectibles—
from the magnificent to beloved relics*

1905 Emporium Mall, 129
31st Street Antiques 220
The Acorn 60
A Dickens of a Place, 162
American Heritage Antique
   Center, 144
Antiquarians Bldg, 34
Antique Alley , 174
Antique Bazaar, 206
Antique Emporium at the Milk
   Pail, 118
Antique Markets I, II, III, 192
Antique Warehouse, Grayslake, 92
Antiques Center of Illinois, 98
Antiques Centre, The, 32
Antiques, etc., 214
Antiques Mart of Elk Grove
   Village, 110
Antiques on Old Plank Rd, 205
Antiques on the Avenue, 26
Armitage Antique Gallery, 44
At Home with Antiques &
   Collectibles, 216
Banowetz Antique Mall, 147
Batavia Antique Shops, 198
Beacon Avenue Dealers, 230
Benson Corners Back Door
   Antique Mall, 157
Cambridge Antique Mall, 183
Carriage Antiques, 123
Crete-Beecher, 238
Dairy Barn Antiques, 132
Delafield Antiques Center, 163
Delavan Antique & Art Centre 172
East State Street Antique Malls 136
Emporium of Long Grove 102
Findings of Geneva 194
Forest Park Antiques, 216
Freddy Bears's Antique Mall, 176
Geneva Antique Market, 194
Grafton Antique Mall, 169
Hawthorne Antiques & Galleries 154

Heavenly Haven Antique Mall, 177
Hebron, Ill Shops, 130
Heritage Trail Mall, 70
International Antiques Centre, 42
Kenilworth Antiques Center 75
LaGrange Antique Mall, 221
Lake Geneva Antique Mall, 173
Lemont Dealers, 222
Mary's Antique Mall, 208
Memory Merchant, The, 190
Miracle on 58th Street, 152
Morris Antique Emporium, 229
Nana's Cottage, 209
Naperville Antique Mall,202
Oakton Street Antique Centre, 108
On the Square, 175
Oswego Antique Markets, 210
Palatine Antique Centre, 115
Park Avenue Antique Mall, 95
Pennsylvania Place, 189
Penny Lane Antiques, 123
Plano/Rt. 34 Antique Mall, 202
Port Antiques 171
Pulford Opera House, 145
Racine Antique Mall, 153
Richmond Merchants Assoc., 126
Ridgefield, Ill. Antique Shops, 124
Rindfleisch Antiques, 179
Riverside Antiques, 190
Rt. 59 Antique Mall, 202
Shops on Scranton, The, 90
Storm Hall Antique Mall, 156
Three Sisters Antique Mall, 236
Trolley Barn, The, 232
Valenti Antiques, Inc. 154
Village Antique Mall, Inc.,101
Village Green Antique Mall, 184
Volo Antique Malls, 106
Water Street Antique Mall, 240
Wheaton Antique Mall, 202
Williams Bros. 95
Wrigleyville Antique Mall, 53

Antique Centers

A cluster of shops (sometimes it's the entire town) makes
one stop shopping possible.

Advertisers